T0344458

Cheer and Loathing

One of the most acclaimed writers in animation returns with this informal sequel to his previous books on indie animation, *Unsung Heroes of Animation*, *Animators Unearthed*, and *Mad Eyed Misfits*.

In this collection, award-winning writer, Chris Robinson, looks at a wide range of films, topics (sex, censorship, cultural politics, programming, felt, gifs, VR, dogs) and filmmakers (Masaaki Yuasa, Xi Chen, Gil Alkabetz, Jacques Drouin, Bordo, Rosto, Joaquín Cociña, Cristóbal León, George Schwizgebel, Lizzy Hobbs, Andreas Hykade, Leah Shore, and many others).

Eclectic, brief, fiery, and opinionated, Robinson's gonzo-tinged writing will amuse, confuse, annoy, and maybe even inspire while, hopefully introducing readers to the wonders of independently-produced animation.

The Focus Animation Series aims to provide unique, accessible content that may not otherwise be published. We allow researchers, academics, and professionals the ability to quickly publish high impact, current literature in the field of animation for a global audience. This series is a fine complement to the existing, robust animation titles available through CRC Press/Focal Press.

Series Editor Chris Robinson is the Artistic Director of the Ottawa International Animation Festival (OIAF) and is a well-known figure in the animated film world. We welcome any submissions to help grow the wonderful content we are striving to provide to the animation community.

Cheer and Loathing

Scattered Ramblings on Indie Animation

Chris Robinson

CRC Press
Taylor & Francis Group
Boca Raton London New York

CRC Press is an imprint of the
Taylor & Francis Group, an **informa** business

First edition published 2024
by CRC Press
2385 NW Executive Center Drive, Suite 320, Boca Raton FL 33431

and by CRC Press
4 Park Square, Milton Park, Abingdon, Oxon, OX14 4RN

CRC Press is an imprint of Taylor & Francis Group, LLC

ISBN: 9781032683669 (hbk)
ISBN: 9781032683812 (pbk)
ISBN: 9781032683782 (ebk)

DOI: 10.1201/9781032683782

Typeset in Times New Roman
by Deanta Global Publishing Services, Chennai, India

*"I have no taste for either poverty or honest labor,
so writing is the only recourse left for me"*

– Hunter S. Thompson

*"Proud Highway: Saga of a Desperate
Southern Gentleman, 1955-1967,"*

For Harrison Neall

Contents

About the Author

Chris Robinson is a Canadian writer and author. He is also the Artistic Director of the Ottawa International Animation Festival (OIAF) and is a well-known figure in the animated film world and was recently given the 2020 award for Outstanding Contribution to Animation Studies by the World Festival of Animation Film - Animafest Zagreb. In 2022, Robinson received the Prix Rene Jodoin for his contributions to Canadian Animation.

Robinson has been called "one of the stylistically most original and most provocative experts in the history of animation. He made a name for himself with a unique and eclectic magazine column *Animation Pimp*, which became a book of the same name (the column was later renamed into *Cheer and Loathing in Animation*).

Mastering different methods and styles in critical and scholarly approaches, Robinson covers a broad range of Canadian and global subject matters in his books *Estonian Animation: Between Genius and Utter Illiteracy*, *Unsung Heroes of Animation*, *Canadian Animation: Looking for a Place to Happen*, *Ballad of a Thin Man: In Search of Ryan Larkin*, *Animators Unearthed*, *Japanese Animation: Time out of Mind* and Mad Eyed Misfits: Writings on Indie Animation

Robinson's most recent animation writing includes *Earmarked for Collision*, the first ever history of collage animation. He is currently writing *Dreaming a Way (of) Life*, a book about the legendary collage filmmaker, Lewis Klahr (CRC Press, 2024).

In addition to his writing on animation, Robinson also wrote the Award-winning animated short, *Lipsett Diaries* (2010) directed by Theodore Ushev. He recently completed the illustrated novel *My Balls are Killing Me* with artist, Andreas Hykade, and wrote the script for *Idling,* a live-action feature directed by Theodore Ushev.

Introduction

In 2006 or thereabouts, I put out a book called *Unsung Heroes of Animation*. In 2010, came *Animators Unearthed*. In 2022, came *Mad Eyed Misfits*. These books contain my words and thoughts on assorted independent animation artists, and individual films. The purpose? Well, first, it allows me to gather my many varied writings under one roof. More importantly, it carries on the mission to keep spreading the word about these under-the-radar artists who continue to largely be ignored by both the general public and the art scene. That's just the way it is with indie animation. The public wants digestible fast food with talking animals and linear narratives. Indie animation is deemed too 'weird' and 'arty', yet the art gallery scene doesn't think animation is 'arty' enough. Well, tough beans for both of them. Indie animation doesn't need you. It's like a small self-sufficient community. We're getting on just fine.

So then, *Cheer and Loathing* (yes, the title is loosely inspired by Hunter S. Thompson's "Fear and Loathing.") collects my assorted animated musings from 2013-2023. The pieces vary in tone, style and quality. Some are accessible profiles, others are intentionally freewheeling rants. Basically, I write to find out what I think about something. If you're looking for 'deep' academic writing, you won't find that here. Honestly, I rarely even read books about animation. I've always been more influenced by explosive and provocative writings of old music critics like Richard Meltzer and Nick Tosches, the New Journalism style of the 1960s/1970s, and the mischievousness of Andy Kaufman. I've never understood or liked those dry, supposedly objective writings by academics or journalists. So boring. Objectivity is a cop-out. You gotta dive in there with everything you've lived and breathed. To leave 'you' out of a writing is absurd, wrong and downright sad.

I want to thank Dan Sarto (Animation World Network) and Amid Amidi (Cartoon Brew) for allowing me to reprint assorted articles that I originally wrote for their online publications. Second, thanks to the folks at Sight and Sound magazine who, for a while, let me write for them.

Thank you to every animator included in this book.

Chris Robinson

A Boy and His Atom (2013)

1

On its surface, the one-minute animation film *A Boy and His Atom* doesn't look like anything special or new. Composed entirely of what appear to be silver balls, it shows a boy dancing and playing with a silver ball before he tosses it into the sky where it forms the word "Think."

Insert slow, sarcastic 'golf clap' after the film ends.

A Boy and His Atom looks like it could be a high-school film, a lost Norman McLaren or René Jodoin experiment from the early days of the National Film Board of Canada (NFB) or a variation of the 1970s video game PONG.

Look deeper, though – 100 million times or so – and you'll spot something astonishing about this film: *The Boy and His Atom* was made entirely out of atoms by a team of IBM scientists.

The folks at Guinness – the records people, not the brewers, have officially deemed it The World's Smallest Stop-Motion Film. Okay, I change my golf clap to a full clap accompanied by a wide-eyed look of astonishment.

The atoms were manipulated using a device called a Scanning Tunnelling Microscope (STM) – which sounds like something a proctologist will be using on me in the future. The STM, whose development earned a couple of IBM eggheads a Nobel Prize in Physics in 1986, is described "as a needle that drags atoms across a surface using magnetism." A copper plate was used as the surface of the animation while carbon monoxide provided the most stable atoms for animating.

Pretty impressive – nay, mind-blowing – stuff (IBM has since done some *Star Trek*-related pieces as well), but what does it mean for animation?

A Boy and His Atom follows in a long tradition of collaborations between animation and science. In fact, one of the first computer-animation films, *Hunger* (Peter Foldes, 1974), was made collaboration between the aforementioned NFB and scientists at the National Research Council of Canada. While *A Boy...* is a nifty little experiment that expands animation's technical arsenal, will it have any significant impact on animation? IBM scientists seem more interested in using the movie as a way of promoting IBM and having a bit of fun with their STM. Hopefully, the response to the film will encourage them to seek out animation artists to collaborate on more enriching and stimulating works of art.

DOI: 10.1201/9781032683782-1

She Can Fly Anything Right

The Golden Touch of Marcy Page (2014)

2

In preparation for a retirement shindig being held for animation producer, Marcy Page, at the National Film Board of Canada (NFB) in Montreal, I was putting together a small tribute on behalf of the Ottawa International Animation Festival (OIAF). We'd decided to make up a small scroll containing all the films that Marcy has produced that have screened at the OIAF. Travelling down her production trail is like scanning over the roster of the Montreal Canadiens dynasties of the 1950s and 1970s. It is littered with all-stars: *Ryan, The Danish Poet, Madame Tutli-Putli, Subconscious Password, Wild Life, Flux, The End of the World in Four Seasons, How Wings are Attached to the Back of Angels* and on and on. Even more impressive is the Hall of Fame roster behind these films: Chris Landreth, Chris Hinton, Amanda Forbis & Wendy Tilby, Craig Welsh, Janet Perlman, Don McWilliams, Paul Driessen, Torill Kove etc.… So, just how did a converted Californian end up becoming Canadian animation's golden girl?

"While I was teaching animation production and animation history classes at San Francisco State University," says Page, "my teaching partner, Marty McNamara and I taught some intensive "Focus" classes, including some on the films of the NFB. We were able to get 16mm prints from the local Canadian Consulate and they also generously helped by flying in special guests for these classes. As a result, we met a lot of enormously talented Canadian animation directors."

Impressed by the strong soundtracks of Canadian animation films, Page and McNamara approached the Consulate about bringing in a composer they

DOI: 10.1201/9781032683782-2

both admired. "[Paul Driessen's] *An Old Box*," adds Page, "was one of my favorite films at the time and we also very much admired *The Sweater* and *Crac*, so we decided on the composer we saw in the credits, Normand Roger."

Roger agreed and presented his work in San Francisco. McNamara then convinced Page to show Roger parts of *Paradisia* (1987), a film she was animating at the time, in front of a production class so that they could show students a sample first encounter between a director and a composer.

The presentation went so well that Page felt confident enough to approach Roger to ask him if he would compose the music for *Paradisia*. Roger's response would change the course of Page's life.

"Normand kindly agreed and when the film was ready for post, I came to Montreal for the final phases of the sound production. After the film was mixed and I felt elated and released from the bondage of a long production, it was also easy to notice that Normand was a very charming man. Ultimately, he asked me if I might consider moving to Montreal."

She did.

Fittingly, the Californian arrived during a typically brisk Canadian winter in 1988. "Since I fell in love in (and with) Montreal during the summer, it was sobering to actually move here in the middle of January. Normand took me straight from the airport to La Baie and got me a big coat and warm boots."

Culturally, the adjustment wasn't as challenging as one might imagine for an unilingual Californian transplant.

> "Many of my ancestors," says Page, were coincidentally French Canadian, so despite being disdainfully *American* or bizarrely *Californian*, I am secretly 'pure laine' – unfortunately the ability to speak French is not genetically encoded. There were some family memories, passed down from my grandmother, that I finally understood. Still, I am clearly a cultural transplant. Fortunately, Canada has lots of immigrants. Being an outsider, in voluntary exile, is however not a bad place to consider artistic culture.

And what's an immigrant animator to do in Montreal? Well, work for the NFB, naturally. "While I was endlessly waiting for my landed immigrant status," recalls Page, "then NFB producer David Verrall ominously invited me for lunch one day and asked me about my future career plans."

"I had seen *Paradisia*," says Verrall, "and in truth more than one person mentioned to me I should meet this new talent in town. In particular, Wendy Tilby – who had met Marcy somewhere – urged me to at least meet Marcy."

On the day that Page got her landed immigrant status in 1990, Verrall presented her with a mini Canadian flag and immediately hired her to direct/animate and associate-produce for an NFB documentary on palaeontology. "I was in the midst of a complicated co-production with," recalls Verrall,

PBS, a Canadian indie company and as I recall Japanese partners on a dinosaur doc for which we were to provide all the animation sequences of dinosaurs imagined. I already had a bunch of animation talent engaged – there were still some staff animator directors at that time – but not enough creative leads in play for every segment. So, my offer to Marcy once she was legit to work in Canada was for a directing/animating role in the studio particular to this big co-pro.

While Verrall was impressed with Page's design and animation work on the project, he had even greater respect for how well she worked with other animators. What Marcy refers to as associate producing was much less formal.

This involved my observation that Marcy was a natural (producing-wise) that other players gravitated to her for advice and encouragement and, best for me, that advice and encouragement generally led not just to better work by those seeking it but contributed materially to actually getting the work done and out.

So impressed was Verrall that he "became determined to woo this talented animator/director towards the less certain pleasures of producing."

With Eunice Macaulay on the verge of retiring as a producer, the timing was perfect. Boosted by the encouragement of animator John Weldon, Page applied for the job, got the job, and, well, the rest is animation history.

While Page acknowledges that making the adjustment from animator to producer was difficult, she was philosophical about the change: "The arithmetic is better. Some animation directors can only count the short films they can create in a lifetime on their fingers. As a producer, you can touch a lot more productions, though arms' length is a long distance."

David Verrall, though, recalls that the discussion with Page about redirecting her career

was much more consequential as I remember it. There is no doubt this will have deprived the world of some personal films from Marcy's hand but (as I am an unapologetic advocate for the crucial symbiotic role of Producer beside Key Creator) I say this choice was the greater good.

Few will disagree. Actually, I'd be hard pressed to find a single person who would quarrel with this decision.

Page admits that even now she does miss the direct thrill of animating.

Animating is such a powerful kick. I still remember vividly seeing my first animation exercises move on film. Such a miracle to make something come to life like that. Maybe I will find it in me again... if I can forget the arithmetic.

Leaving animating behind is one thing, but how does one just become a producer – especially with minimal experience? "I suppose I tried," says Page, "to channel the lessons of my father, Jerry Page, who was an educator and whose style of leadership was about coaxing others to find their own voice, their point of view, their faith in their own abilities – always a paradox as when it worked the best it was often the most invisible." Page also tried to imagine what she would have needed in a producer when she was a director.

When you look at the diversity of directors, techniques, and films Page has produced, one word comes to mind: eclectic.

> I love the many ways that animation present itself, so the variety of what appeals to me is hard to pin down. I remember [American animator] Sara Petty once telling me that when she makes a film, she has an audience she keeps in her head of about a dozen people... and half of them are dead artists. I agree that creating (or seeking out) animation is a conversation with, among other things, the history of art and film. The audience, living and dead, that I keep in my own head has grown over the years.

Page's productions have straddled the borders of linear and experimental narratives. Well, she admits to loving "a well-told story" that has touches of pathos, irony, humour, vitality and the ability to surprise (e.g., *The Danish Poet*, *Dinner for Two*, *Snow Cat*), Page is also smitten by more experimental approaches like those of Paul Driessen, Craig Welch or Chris Hinton's wonderful film, *Flux*. "I like," Page adds,

> the visual games of Paul Driessen that with each project seem to invent new rules to expand cinematic language. When Chris Hinton proposed *Flux*, it was the appeal of a film that just bordered on comprehension but that pushed all the edges toward abstraction.

Another characteristic of Page's productions is their innovative and striking graphics. "I am attracted to compelling visual style like the graphic mastery/mystery of Craig Welch who fearlessly visited the dark side with his *How Wings Are Attached to the Backs of Angels*," says Page.

> Or the under-camera moving paintings of Lynn Smith, each image so luscious that you wanted to lick the paint... or the inventive mixtures of abstract and recognizable form in the work of Malcolm Sutherland... or the completely entrancing otherworldly creations of the "Clyde Henrys" (Chris Lavis and Maciek Szczerbowski). One look at their sympathetic heroine (*Madame Tutli-Putli*) standing with all her meager possessions waiting for the train and I was ready to take the ride. Chris Landreth's visual style ('psycho-realism') transcended the eye candy of most CG work of the time and he was passionate about ideas, the perfect blend of medium and message. Wendy

> Tilby and Amanda Forbis too seem, in the balance of their mammoth talents to always put forth a perfect union of art and idea, visual and sound.

And what about the personalities behind these creations? Just how important is it for a producer to have some familiarity with the filmmaker or to at least be able to manage hotheaded and fragile egos (which, admittedly, are few and far between in animation – at least by comparison to their live-action compatriots.) "Animation filmmakers are as various in their personalities as their art forms," admits Page.

> They seem genuinely appreciative of anyone who can articulate just how amazing their work is. They are, as a group, quite exemplary – funny, smart, humble and kind. The easiest part of my job was in being an advocate for these extraordinary people.

Of course, a producer can't just sit back and stroke their filmmakers' egos. They have to be able to give honest feedback no matter how difficult it might be for a filmmaker to hear. That requires time and trust. When talking to a number of filmmakers who worked with Page, it's clear that they had complete trust in her approach.

"When I worked with Marcy," says Malcolm Sutherland (*Forming Games*), "there was a sense of openness, as if anything were possible. She is patient and has a great sense of the long view. Marcy was very hands off, unless you asked for her help. For me this was ideal."

Marcy is good at many things," says Torill Kove (*My Grandmother Ironed the King's Shirts*, *The Danish Poet*) "but I think for me personally, her unique contribution is her trust. It's like any other close relationship where you are left alone to be who you are. It is liberating."

"Marcy," adds Munro Ferguson (*Falling in Love Again*)

> was the best producer I ever worked with. Her method was simple. She would find a director that she really believed in and then back them 100%. She brought to the table wisdom, humor and sensitivity. Her approach was nurturing. And she has the gift of a beautiful, calm voice which could the sooth nerves of the most freaked-out director.

Building a trusting relationship first requires being able to have faith in oneself. That inner trust takes time and experience to find. "Overall," adds Page,

> I suppose I've learned more to trust my instincts – some inner barometer of passion – when you feel something is the right risk to take. Is it finally only the risky projects that make sense to pursue? It is not always possible and of course one can deceive oneself, but when it works, the conversation in your head with that internal audience and all those dead artists is worth it!

Okay… so…it's some 23 years later and Marcy Page is closing the door on a remarkably rich period of her life. I asked her what have been the most invaluable things she's taken from her NFB experience. Surprisingly, her first response was connected with technical stuff: "Some small words of advice… given the company I keep [i.e.i.e., Normand Roger, in case you forgot already, dear reader], I've learned a lot more about the relationship of sound to image in filmmaking over the years. I know now that while one can often consciously excuse an incomplete or rough visual assembly, that sound tends to act on us more unconsciously. We won't realize that it is a rough track or incomplete mix but more likely we will say that it is just a bad film. It is very, very important to get the relationship to sound right and that it conspire in the novelty and innovation of the work."

That's it? Come on Marcy! Give us something sexier.

> The big takeaway for me is that I really do have fondness and respect for the people with whom I've worked all these years. That has always made any trouble fade to insignificance. The NFB is a miraculous, improbable institution built on the pioneering dedication and creativity of decades of such people. I hope it outlives us and our children's children. As we near the 100th anniversary of the birth of Norman McLaren, whose founding vision for the Animation program there, still informs the producers who follow me, it seems important not to take it for granted.

Take note Canadian taxpayers and Government funders.

Marcy Page's retirement is a huge loss for animation, not just because of her golden touch as a producer, but because she is one of the most genuinely good people in our little world. When I stumbled into animation not long after Page joined the NFB, I was lured less by the films than by the generosity and openness of the people creating them. Marcy Page is one of the good souls that I've encountered and quietly admired beneath the unpolished veneer of my apparent bad-boy image. Her positivity, calm and compassionate nature, warm, and slightly sly, smile, along with her unabashed love for animation and its creators is something that we will all sorely miss. There will always be more great animation films, but there will never be another Marcy Page.

You Look Like Me by Pierre Hébert (2015)

3

During his long career making animated films for the National Film Board of Canada (NFB), Pierre Hébert was known for his abstract experimental work *Op Hop* and *Around Perception*, along with social/politically charged films (e.g., *La Plante Humaine, Memories of War*). Hébert retired from the NFB in 1999 but carried on as an independent animator continuing to explore and expand his interest in experimentation through live animation performances, cross-discipline collaborations, live-action/animation hybrids (e.g., *Thunder Road*) and time-lapse video installations. His latest film, *You Look Like Me*, is an inspired collaborative effort that fuses all of Hébert's long-standing themes while bridging both narrative and abstract techniques.

The roots of *You Look Like Me* are also quite multi-layered. A Quebec children's TV writer, Paule Marier, wrote the original text. In 2014, her partner, Quebec musician René Lussier (whom Hébert had collaborated with in the 1980s) turned the text into a song. Then another Quebec musician, Jim Corcoran recorded the text in English for a radio show he hosted. Corcoran then sent the English version back to Lussier and suggested he create new music over the re-recorded text. Lussier obliged. After listening to the soundtrack, the duo felt that images would enhance the work.

Hello Pierre Hébert.

Hébert received the work as a completed soundtrack and was instantly attracted to the balance of the text, narration and music along with the social and political themes that paralleled strands of his own films.

Hébert, though, didn't start from scratch (see… that was a pun). The images, like the text and music came out of a long process. He'd been animating heads and faces in a series of live performances called *Tropismes*. Hébert then took a series of drawings used in *You Look Like Me* from video captures of different *Tropismes* performances. The extracts from Tropismes were then added on top of new drawings. According to Hébert, "*You Look Like Me* either took three months or three years. It came from a long process but the final work was quick."

DOI: 10.1201/9781032683782-3

You Look Like Me captures the struggle to recollect and reconstruct a fleeting encounter into a tangible memory. Through a memory of the eyes, the narrator puts together a picture not of one image, but an entire world, not of one boy (incredibly, the final image was not the inspiration for the original text), but of humanity. The result is a staggering and affecting work that touches on loss, exile, identity, and memory.

Au Hazard Bear Another *by Sean Buckelew (2014)*

4

Sometime in June, I was in the midst of screening 2,000 submissions to the Ottawa International Animation Festival. Up popped an undergraduate film called *Another*. The running time says 17 minutes. "Sweet fuck," I thought. At least this will be quick and relatively painless, 'cause 299 times out of 300 they stink. If you're making a 17-minute film, it best be a masterpiece. If you're a student making a 17-minute film, well, just don't. Just stop right now.

The film starts. Surprisingly, it's hand-drawn with coloured pencil. You don't see that too often nowadays (though the director, Sean Buckelew, is a student of the fine Chicago animator Chris Sullivan). Visually, I feel like I'm watching a lost student film from the 1980s.

I keep watching.

Next thing I know… the end credits are rolling.

What the hell just happened?

If Bresson's donkey in *Au Hasard Balthazar* was a symbol of Christ-like suffering and cruelty, then Buckelew's bear might be a stand-in for *Cape Fear*'s Max Cady, a cold, mean, psychotic killer, yet one who becomes accepted, loved and grieved for by the mother and son.

The narrative is so free-flowing and straightforward it can be approached and interpreted in any number of ways. Is this a metaphor for domestic violence? Did this once gentle father turn into a cold, abusive beast? Do the boy and mother accept the bear into their existence out of desperation? Is it just a silly film about what it would be like if a bear lived in a human marriage? Is the bear the actual victim, a prisoner of these strange, desperately lonely and grieving humans?

While the scenes are ordinary and uneventful – although they are funny at times; the paw-shaped door handle, the bear swatting the bedroom lamp

10   DOI: 10.1201/9781032683782-4

off – Buckelew's elliptical narrative, tightly framed shots and use of music (notably Beethoven's *Piano Sonata No. 25*) create a mysterious and tense setting that leaves you on edge. We're never really sure what the hell is going on, let alone what will happen next.

Death's stench seeps through the pours of the cabin waiting to pounce. And we know it will because it always does. But what surprises here – and what makes *Another* such a rich, satisfying and unusual work – is not death itself, but life's reaction to it.

Pig by Steven Subotnick (2015)

5

"The pig is everything," says the synopsis for *Pig* (2015), a rapid-fire, poetic-comic musing by American independent animator, Steven Subotnick, on the connection between humans and our little pink friends.

"Pigs carry many connotations," says Subotnick. "They are forbidden food in some cultures, savory meals for others, they are animals, and they are like humans. Pigs are also disgusting. They will eat anything, including feces and other dead pigs. In this sense, the pig is everything."

Subotnick found inspiration for the film while listening to pig-calling contests on YouTube (no, I did not ask him *why* he was seeking out pig-calling contests on YouTube). "Both the sound of pig-calling and the intensity of the callers is strange," adds Subotnick. "It's as if the caller becomes a pig." It's this overlap between pig and man that lies at the heart of *Pig*. Considering humanity's endless hunger for *something*, for *anything* to fill some imagined void, we are left to ponder just who the real pig is.

"We are both omnivores, have similar teeth, blood and skin, and are both intelligent," says Subotnick. "The man in the film is empty. The pig is everything to him, and his hunger is so total it goes beyond his body."

Pig features beautifully distorted drawings and paintings, some crisp editing, and hilarious vocal performance by Joel Frenzer, who also did voice work on Subotnick's previous films, *Fight* (2012), *Boy* (2011) and *Jelly Fishers* (2009).

> "I've known Joel for a long time – he was my student at RISD," says Subotnick. "His acting and voice talents were always evident. Joel is inventive, versatile and always enthusiastic. Joel could probably voice a stick, if you asked him. He's a natural storyteller and can use his voice to bring out unusual narrative qualities."

Although Subotnick has been making films for over 20 years, he only made three films between 1994–2004. However, since 2011, Subotnick has had a creative eruption, producing a succession (11 films, to be accurate) of thoughtful, original, mesmerizing animation, shall we say, haikus (most of the films

DOI: 10.1201/9781032683782-5

run under three minutes). "I shifted my focus from trying to make good films – which takes me out of the creative process in order to judge it – to simply creating work," says Subotnick. "This decision gave me the freedom to work quickly and directly. I set strict limitations. For example, to make a film from one image, or one sequence, or within two weeks." A wise choice that has benefited both the artist and the audience.

Paradise Awaits (2015)

6

Polish animator, Tomek Ducki stormed onto the indie animation scene in 2014 with his beautiful, mysterious and haunting meditation on mortality, *Baths*. This year, Ducki returns with *Paradise Awaits*, a neon-drenched old-testament-tinged music video made for electronic artist, Zhu. It features a singing, swirling, animation-leaking head, a naked lady, a mysterious square apple, pixilated fig leaves and some delicious dripping dances of paint that transform Eden from sin bin into a cool, chill-out space.

Zhu's manager approached Ducki after seeing *My Turn*, the young Polish animator's video for the electronic music duo, Basement Jaxx. Initially, Ducki wasn't sure that he'd be a good match but decided to give it a try. "There was something intriguing about potentially working for an artist who is completely invisible and only put out one video so far. This meant that I would have a chance to explore a new visual language and persona."

Still, falling in love with the project was a long process.

> The subjects, the Biblical themes and the music, it all seemed so distant from each other. While the technique (a rather complex layering of CGI, 2D drawn and vector-based graphics that were then painted over frame by frame) helped us to connect all these distant worlds in a visual sense, it took some risky experimentation to find the right balance. The first scene that really got me going was the cubic apple hanging and swinging around the girl's head as Zhu sings, "I have seen your face".

Using Titian's famous painting (*The Temptation of Adam and Eve*) as a reference (it's featured on the song's cover art), Ducki offers a fresh take on the whole Adam and Eve shenanigans. "I was interested, in how the fruit of the tree of knowledge changes the vision of the first people." So once Eve takes the square apple (which looks suspiciously like LSD tabs) into her mouth, the freewheeling sinuous imagery shifts into rigid pixilated fig-leaf squares (fig leaves are used in Titian's painting to hide the naughty bits). The squares have taken over. The party, it seems, is over.

DOI: 10.1201/9781032683782-6

Paradise Awaits took Ducki and his team of seven people about two exhausting months from concept to sign-off.

> I landed super sick in the bed by the very end, but it was worth it because we got to experiment a lot with animation and movement and play and explore a visual narration of associations of shapes and symbols, movements and rhythm.

Nuggets by Andreas Hykade (2015)

7

One of the things that first attracted me to animation was the economy and deceptive simplicity of the best films. As a Film Studies student, I'd grown accustomed to weighty concepts being handed out methodically – and sometimes painfully (e.g., Antonioni, Akerman) – over a period of 90–120 minutes. So when I first stumbled upon some short animation works that crammed a wealth of ideas and emotions into 5–6 minutes, it was, well, mind-blowing. It's not a knock-on feature film. I liken it to music. The Who, for example, made a couple of ambitious concept albums (*Tommy*, *Quadrophenia*) that could also just as easily be summed up in a couple of brilliant Pete Townshend songs, *Misunderstood* and *The Real Me*. Sometimes just a song is enough.

Which brings me to German animator, Andreas Hykade. I tend to liken his work to that of a musician partially because we've talked and shared music a fair bit over the years. He's like an old bluesman of animation, creating these seemingly simple narratives rife with pain and experience.

Early on in his career, Hykade veered towards the concept album approach with two larg-scale – and exceptional – films (*We Lived in Grass*, *Ring of Fire*) that delved into masculinity, sexuality, mortality, family and violence. After *Ring of Fire*, Hykade stepped back and produced smaller-scale films (e.g., *The Runt*, *Love and Theft*) music videos, and a clever children's TV series, *Tom*) that were just as effective conceptually as his longer films.

Ironically, *Nuggets* originally started, Hykade tells me, "as a big epic thing", but a health scare put that project on hold. Forced to stay in a hospital after undergoing surgery to determine whether he had cancer or not, an anxious, frustrated Hykade called his studio (Film Bilder) and asked them to bring over some paper and a lightbox. He spent the next 10 days creating the drawings for *Nuggets*. By the time he was discharged from the hospital and given a clean bill of health, he returned to the studio and – with a small team of six people – completed the film.

16

DOI: 10.1201/9781032683782-7

Using just a single line, a Kiwi bird, an egg and a disarming 'cartoony' visual style, Hykade creates a powerful and straightforward depiction of the genesis and evolution of addiction. The film's vagueness (is the egg Heroin? Booze?) is also its strength. You don't have to be an alcoholic or drug addict to understand the message. The egg could be a metaphor for anything in life: coffee, smoking, eating, TV, Internet, or mobile phones. In fact, Hykade's illustration of addiction is so clear and concise that children and teenagers would benefit from being exposed to the film.

Given the circumstances of its creation, *Nuggets* can also be read as a metaphor for life. Life can start out so pleasantly and trouble free, but as we go on we often stumble into more unpleasantness and more problems.

Creation Myth (2015)

8

While the last year has produced some spectacular animated music videos (e.g., *Moving On, Unity),* the genre has historically been very erratic. Sometimes the animation dazzles but the song stinks; and vice-versa. A common misstep made by many a young animator is a lack of intimacy or cohesion between image and sound. With some videos, you get the sense that animation and music are strangers, having only just met in post-production. Too often, the music seems like it was tossed onto the soundtrack of a pre-existing animation.

Not so with Angela Stempel's *Creation Myth.* From that first blast of guitar, the animation jumps right on board like an old friend. And in a sense, it was. Stempel was a fan of the band (Celestial Shore) long before she made the video. "I met the band," says Stempel, "through friends and going to shows in New York where they are based.

It was one of the band members who initially approached Stempel about making a music video. "It was a very casual," Stempel recalls. "Oh, you should make a video for us. I always responded to their music, so for me it was an incredible opportunity to illustrate the complexity of their sound through a variety of mediums and experiments."

Just as *Creation Myth* has a Pixies/Guided by Voices, garage band/lo-fi feel, Stempel's mix of contemporary and traditional (cut-out) animation techniques gives the video an old-school vibe.

> I love the look of real textures, and working through the limitations of a certain technique. The looks of the 2D bits of the film are inspired by traditional cel animation. The cut-out work I made using a series of photographs and textured paper. There are so many possibilities with replacement animation, and it always just looks so good.

Stempel's interpretation of the song's evolution-inspired lyrics is also unique and playful, and in fact, almost seems to argue that we're devolving.

> I was inspired by the way people on television always look 'better' than in real life. The plot unravels though, the way it does for nature, and gets out of the protagonist's control, when he stops wanting to 'evolve' any further.

DOI: 10.1201/9781032683782-8

I don't know if I'm evolving or devolving, but I do know that *Creation Myth* is a delirious, heart-pumping, head-shaking fireworks feast of colour, rhythm, crunchy guitars and dizzying animation.

Dig it.

Small People with Hats (2015) 9

A cross-continental jaunt between Japan and London via Estonia, Sarina Nihei's Royal College of Art graduate film, *Small People with Hats* has had a polarizing existence on the animation festival circuit. Despite winning Grand Prizes at the Ottawa and Holland Animation Festivals, the Japanese native's hypnotic and absurdist tale about a possibly evil group of identical small people with – you guessed it – hats, has also been rejected by a number of festivals and criticized as a hollow copy of the style and feel of Estonian animation.

There is no doubting the Estonian influence. From the minimalist design and movement to the deadpan characters and absurdist situations, *Small People with Hats* wouldn't look out of place on the roster of Estonia's Joonisfilm studio. Nor does Nihei deny the Estonian influence.

> I've been influenced by Priit Pärn's work because he always has strong ideas in terms of making a film, which includes satire and humour. I think I like to see black elements in films but still entertaining. Also, I just found Estonian language and culture intriguing.

Nihei's Estonian crush is by no means unique. The Eesti touch, so to speak (which is really a fusion of Monty Python, Jean-Luc Godard, Pop-Art and Buster Keaton, sprinkled with a pinch of Soviet oppression) has influenced numerous animation short films (notably a chunk of Japanese student animation in recent years) and even some American TV shows (including 1990s kids' series, *Rugrats* and *Aaahh!!! Real Monsters*!, along with more adult fare like *Superjail).*

What's the appeal? Likely the way Estonian artists almost always take on heavy themes (e.g., politics, identity) with a smart and dark sense of humour (something sorely lacking in animation today). As American comedian Louis CK once said, "Everything that's difficult you should be able to laugh about."

Small People with Hats, with its cast of cold Keatonesque assholes and comic scenes of bloodshed, murder and betrayal certainly fits the bill. But this is more than just a clever Estonian cover song. Nihei's ambiguous narrative (are the small people with hats the villains imposing their will or are they, in

DOI: 10.1201/9781032683782-9

fact, the ones being imprisoned and brainwashed?) is complemented by crisp, surprising edits (that simultaneously generate humour, horror and mystery, while poking the audience to keep up) and an innovative and expressive sound design (a rare feat in this era of talk/music drenched animation) that is so vibrant it becomes a character of its own.

Old Man (2016)

10

I've never fully understood the fascination with Charles Manson. He wasn't the first, second or last mass murderer in human history. Perhaps it's because the Manson murders signified (symbolically at least) the end of the 1960s, the hippies and all that so-called peace, love and understanding stuff. It's also a reflection of our own fascination with human darkness. We're all an unharmonious mix of light and dark. Sometimes one overshadows the other. Rarely does one take over the other, at least to a Manson-like extreme. So, when we have an opportunity to take a peek inside the mind of someone who has gone over that so-called edge, we grab it.

That brings me to Leah Shore's short, *Old Man*, a brash and raunchy impressionistic portrait of Manson as an old man.

After a screening of her student film, *Meatwaffle* at the Sundance festival, a producer approached Shore with an opportunity to make a film based on unreleased phone conversations between Manson and a Canadian writer named Marlin Marynick.

Shore spent three months editing hours of recordings down to five minutes. She then spent another two years animating. The result is a whirling, manic visualization of Manson's freewheeling thoughts on life's big questions: religion, humanity, power, good and evil, and… air. Yes, air.

Manson's freewheeling rants are gold for an inspired young animator like Shore. Her array of animation techniques and drawing styles are perfect companions to Manson's rambling, wide-ranging monologues.

From the title (the ambiguous *Old Man*) to the character design (Manson's face is replaced throughout the film – at least until the end credits – by a scribbly black mass), Shore tries her best to be non-judgmental and to separate Charles Manson the myth from some crazy, rambling old guy: "I wanted to make it as non-judgmental as possible, says Shore, "though, admittedly, I edited the audio, so there is some bias inherent in that, and let the viewer decide if what Manson is say, is 'sane' or 'good' or 'insane' or 'bad.'"

She doesn't quite pull that off though. In the first frame, we're told that these conversations are Manson's. It might have been more interesting to hold off revealing this until the end credits. That way the audience's reactions

DOI: 10.1201/9781032683782-10

toward the character and his thoughts might be more conflicted. Do we give more (or less) credence to his words solely because we know it's Manson? How would we have responded if they were just the words of some anonymous old guy?

It's clearly been impossible for many viewers to take a distance from Manson. "There is some significant portion of the audience," says Shore, "that sees 'Charles Manson' and reflectively hate it, or hate me. It's hard for anyone, to see it as what I intended: an art piece and character analysis."

The reaction to *Old Man* is almost worthy of a story in itself. While the film has received a lot of positive press, it has also generated a lot of vitriolic responses, harassment and racist slurs. Given the dearth of attention indie animation receives, I guess you have to take what you can get.

Horse (2016) 11

Despite China's rich animation history (notably via the Shanghai Animation studio), the country was relatively non-existent (thanks in large part to censorship) on the international animation scene until the digital era. But really, it's only been in the last 5–6 years that some truly inspired and eclectic short films have emerged out of China. Led by, among others, newcomers like Lei Lei (*This is Love*, *Recycled*), Xi Chen & Xu An (*The Sparrow*) Xue Geng (*Mr. Sea*), the Chinese animation scene is coming to life again with works that are beautiful, haunting, graphically innovative and conceptually complex. Among those new voices is Shen Jie whose film, *Horse*, mesmerized the international festival scene in recent years.

With dashes of *Rashomon*, Tarantino, Muybridge and the work of German animator Gil Alkabetz (*Yankale*), this befuddling, hilarious and rapid-fire amphetamine-inspired brainteaser serves up the story of a horse in five cut-up chapters.

Jen, who works for an advertising company, used a finger paint tool in Photoshop ("because sometimes I make films secretly during my work time") to create about 400 individual drawings. Each image was put in sequence before being cut apart and re-edited.

The soundtrack, made by Takanari Sakuma, seamlessly mirrors the fragmented imagery while adding an aura of suspense and overall loopiness to the proceedings.

Now, I've probably seen this film at least a half-dozen times, but I'm still not entirely sure exactly what the hell is going on except that there's a horse, a gun, a horse referee (or a man with a horse mask) and a couple of boxers (who at one time might have shared a horse costume). You know what? It doesn't really matter. Sometimes it's best to just enjoy life without always trying to decipher it.

That said, this refreshing piece of minimalism, with its varying speeds and cut-up imagery, toys with the sensory perceptions of audiences, almost insisting that they are engaged with the screen. Even though they might not find any deep meaning in *Horse*, it will leave them buzzing.

 DOI: 10.1201/9781032683782-11

Do the Collapse *The Night of the Carrots by Priit Pärn (2016)*

12

I love blackouts. There was a pretty sizeable one back in Ottawa (and other parts of Canada and the Eastern U.S.) in August 2003. No internet. No TV. Minimal radio. No video games. Kids played freely in the streets. Neighbours sat out front on their lawn chairs and spoke, drank and ate with each other. Life slowed down, became quieter. Sure, it helped that it was summer, but even when were hit with an ice storm that crippled power during the winter of 1998, there was a certain peace of mind and being that came with it. Life was already noisy back then and it's grown even louder now, "louder than bombs" as the Manchester wit said. I crave more blackouts and suspect that given our drunk-like thirst for energy we'll start enduring more sooner rather than later. Sure, we could choose to have our own blackouts but let's face it we're weak… we're all plugged in, attached to devices, junkies, the lot of us. Facebook, when I'm calm, detached and objective, offers my life very little, yet I check in constantly… almost mechanically… just to see if someone liked something I said… if even that… I'm not even sure just why I check in… maybe it's just to avoid real connection… it really has just become a bad habit… like fondling your balls (granted, if I hadn't I wouldn't have caught my ball cancer early, so that's not the best example)… every so often I want to cancel my account yet always find myself sticking with it… this fear maybe that I might miss something or be forgotten. Silly, cause we'll all be forgotten one day.

I just paused to check Facebook.

And of course, we're missing nothing. Sure, it brings us in contact with international friends or family members living in other cities and countries… but it's pretty scant contact… and hell… these days long-distance calls can easily be made for free… yet go and get off Facebook and see how quiet it

DOI: 10.1201/9781032683782-12

gets... it's like you've gone into exile... you realize that no one emails or calls these days... but I've seen my productivity decrease since the rise of the internet and specifically, of Facebook. I wrote a pile of books between 2003–2010. Nothing since. Sure, part of that is because of changes in my personal life, but some of it is due to procrastinating online.

Remember when we used to read magazines on the toilet?

All the while time is tick tick ticking away. Life is getting shorter. I'm approaching 50 and wondering where the fuck some of my life has gone. Okay...I'm being a tad overdramatic 'cause I'm a bit burnt out and it's hot outside and I think too much, usually about myself. Truthfully, I travel a lot and do a chunk of outdoor activities but take this Facebook stuff away and I bet life tastes even better... Facebook is like a fucking TV dinner of life: instant, tasteless gratification that fleetingly fulfils your appetite only to leave it feeling empty or nauseous soon after. Life... or reality... or direct contact... well that's like a carefully, lovingly prepared multi-course meal.

Which brings me at long last to Priit Pärn's hilarious dose of absurdity, *The Night of the Carrots*, which was made right around the time of the Y2K panic. The Y2K stuff started because computer programmers identified years using only the last two numbers. This meant that went the clock hit midnight to ring in 2000, computers would be so confused (possibly thinking we'd all taken a ride in the Tardis back to 1900 which, would have been pretty cool depending on which Doctor you were saddled with) that they'd shut down, taking the world with it. Planes falling from the sky, financial systems in collapse, dogs barking, babies screaming, men crying, windows breaking. Full-on apocalypse.

Sadly, none of that happened though apparently some slot machines stopped working in Delaware.

Now where were we?

Ah, yes, *The Night of the Carrots*.

You can read the film in many ways. Perhaps it's a commentary on the facile essence of the cult of celebrity (Diego Maradona, Michael Jackson, Mikhail Gorbachev, Helmut Kohl, and Steffi Graf are among those referenced in the film) or is it a cautionary tale about the false allure of free-market economies and the European Union (echoing Pärn's earlier classic, *Hotel E*, which, made as the Soviet Union was crumbling, suggested that life might be different in capitalist countries but not necessarily better). Estonia had only been independent a few years and there were many debates about whether the country would be best served by joining the E.U. or not (they finally did, after much debate, in 2004).

All these interpretations – and there must be others – are valid, but I always see *The Night of the Carrots* as a likeminded spirit aching for the self-destruction of computers and with it the internet and all the other damn things we have hooked up to us like a fucking I.V. bag.

At the core of *The Night of the Carrots* is a sanitarium-like place called 'PGI.' Crowds of people are aching for their chance to get it. It's not entirely clear just why they want in though. The narrator suggests that, "being contenders was their real aim because once they were in, they would have nothing to do."

In each of PGI's rooms we meet a variety of bizarre characters (including Michael the Zebra, a thin, fragile white creature – hence nothing like a zebra – clearly modelled on Michael Jackson who dreams of marrying a hefty lass) who want only to escape. The occupants each have a personal dream that, they soon discover, they cannot realize because they are literally plugged into their rooms.

There is hope though.

During a random night once a year, all the rabbits (who control the world through computers) inexplicably turn into carrots and liberate the occupants of PGI.

Certainly, when read in the context of the Y2K panic, *The Night of the Carrots* seems to celebrate the possibility of temporary liberation from computer systems. Yet, there is much more here. Pärn also voices a prescient commentary on the dangers of allowing technology, internet, and social media to saturate our existence. While they lure you in with the promise of instant, virtual interaction and experiences, they ultimately leave you lonely, longing and disconnected... or something like that.

An Ordinary Blue Monday Morning (2016)

13

It's rare that the animation world sees a film from South Africa that doesn't have the name 'Kentridge' attached to it, so it's nice to see this potent sand-animation debut from Naomi van Niekerk.

Using a poem by Ronelda Kamfer, van Niekerk explores a young girl's innocent preparations for school in a community engulfed by daily violence. The sand animation captures the transitory fragility of daily life in this South African community as Kamfer's text becomes increasingly dark and tragic. We never see the violence, we only hear it recounted in a dry, unemotional tone. This understated approach creates an odd tension while aptly displaying just how common and matter-of-fact murder has become in this community.

"What I liked about the poem," says van Niekerk,

> was the style of the writing, Kamfer's writing manages to convey heart-wrenching stories in a very 'matter-of-fact', undramatic way and it was very different to any other poetry I have read in Afrikaans. I also liked the content – the story of a quite 'normal' day for someone growing up in a ghetto of South Africa.

While van Niekerk did not grow up in a violent neighbourhood, she identified with many aspects of the poem.

> I feel it's important to be able to step into someone else's reality and to imagine it as your own, to show compassion for someone else's story. So even though this story was not mine, I can empathize with her story, it's hard to grow up in South Africa and not have an understanding of violence. Some people manage to live their whole lives behind high walls in protected suburbs and choose to turn a blind eye, though this wasn't the case of my childhood.

DOI: 10.1201/9781032683782-13

Van Niekerk was inspired to give sand animation a whirl after seeing an early Caroline Leaf film, *The Owl and The Goose.*

I knew sand animation was something I had to try. With a bucket with sand and a lightbox, you can create a whole world, the process is very lo-fi and tactile.

It felt like the right medium for the poem because of the recurring theme of light and dark in the text that coincides with the process of animating sand on a lightbox. The content of the story is quite dense, and so was the process of animating the scenes using sand and my fingers.

Teeth (2016)　　**14**

This slithery, grinding, haunting and insane tale by Tom Brown and Daniel Gray (*t.o.m.*, 2007) ingeniously conveys the story of a man's life through the history of his teeth. Combining the pacing of Robert Bresson with the lunatic first-person narrative of Poe, *Teeth* takes us inside the mouth of a deeply troubled individual (voiced to perfection by Richard E. Grant) and society.

"The story was born out of a few different stories and story sketches, says Daniel Gray,

> It went through a few different versions with different tones and moods before it settled on what it became. It was influenced by what the then-new Tory government was doing in the U.K. with austerity, which we thought was a bit narrow in its focus. They were closing libraries, cutting arts funding etc. Basically, they were neglecting services that weren't seen as an obvious benefit to the country. Some of these things are very hard to replace.

The duo had Richard E. Grant on their shortlist from the start but because of their slow work schedule ("we were working between jobs," says Gray), they waited 'till the last minute to approach him. "In the end," adds Gray, "we phoned his agent and asked if we could show him the story. The picture was almost complete then, so it was a pretty pitch and he liked it."

Gray admits they were a bit star-struck initially, but that vanished quickly. "He was like someone you'd love to have as a best Uncle. Directing him was easy. He was a pro and seemed to hear everything we wanted from him. He was not at all intimidating."

Naturally, Gray and Brown did an exhaustive amount of dental research, however, there's a mistake in the film. So, let's have a contest. You find the dental mistake and win... well... when I say 'win,' I mean in terms of respect, admiration and appreciation, not prizes. Good luck to you all.

DOI: 10.1201/9781032683782-14

Peace through poetry

15

Ann Marie Fleming on Window Horses *(2016)*

Window Horses, the poignant and timely new feature from Canadian film-maker Ann Marie Fleming, tells the story of Rosie Ming, a naïve young woman of mixed descent who travels abroad for the first time, to a poetry festival in Iran. Through this initially awkward experience, Rosie discovers the world, her family and herself. *Window Horses* is a touching and timely tale that traces the pain, confusion and wonder of multiculturalism, immigration, cultural stereotypes and identity.

The acclaimed feature is not the Asian-Canadian artist's first feature, let alone her first animation film, yet she's still a relative stranger in the indie animation community, largely because she's roamed freely between writing, live-action, experimental, documentary and animation.

A restless, frantic sort, Fleming has been making films since the 1980s. A graduate of Vancouver's Emily Carr Institute of Art and Design, Fleming's films (e.g., *New Shoes*, *You Take Care Now*, *AMF's Tiresias*, *The Magical Life of Long Tack Sam*) have frequently dealt with issues of family and identity, along with an array of difficult social issues (rape, domestic abuse, the Holocaust).

What makes Fleming's body of work unique (aside from her refusal to be categorised) is her ability to address brutally difficult subjects while somehow maintaining a modicum of humour. Her films rarely suffocate from bleakness. Given the overbearing dreariness of many contemporary animation shorts, animators would do well to take notes from Fleming.

DOI: 10.1201/9781032683782-15

31

You're of mixed heritage and your previous feature (*The Magical Life of Long Tack Sam*) also dealt with multicultural issues. Was *Window Horses* also taken from your own experiences?

I'm Chinese on my mother's side, Australian on my father's side, born in Japan with a Korean birth certificate and a Canadian citizen. That hybridity definitely informs my work and my curiosity about other people's invisible histories and the world in general. All my work comes from my own experiences, in some way – my own stories, stories of the people I've met, things I've seen, where I've been.

Can you talk about the genesis of *Window Horses*?

The idea for *Window Horses* actually started about 20 years ago, when I was in an artists' residency in Stuttgart, staying with poets and writers mainly, and listening to their stories of diaspora – particularly after the Second World War – and how the generations in families often didn't pass on their stories. I took a close friend of mine's difficult relationship with his father as a starting point. I was also struggling to live outside of my own culture and language and became fascinated with the idea of translation and adaptation. So, the story was originally a Canadian/German one, because that's where I was.

How did the final script/version of *Window Horses* compare to the first version?

Of course, there were many revisions from the first version of this script, but once Stickgirl became the central character, it is surprisingly close to the original. I had to lose a lot of details along the way to keep it all moving along. I love the side roads, so to speak.

Why Iran? Why a poetry festival?

I was also introduced to the poetry of Rumi while in Germany, and Iranian cinema oddly, but this film did not take place in Iran until I returned to Vancouver many years later and became aware of the stories of the Iranian diaspora (there is a very large Persian community in Vancouver). Again, a close personal relationship was a trigger. I moved the story to Iran. The main character, Rosie Ming, is a half-Iranian and half-Chinese Canadian Stickgirl. Iran and China are both ancient cultures where the poetry of a millennia ago is still very much alive. Human beings are talking to each other across history in a constantly evolving conversation. I find that idea very powerful. It connects us not just across cultures but across time.

Did you ever travel to Iran? Has *Window Horses* been shown there?

No, I have never been to Iran except in my imagination. People in Iran are aware of it, and the plan is to have it distributed there, but we'll have to see if it happens. I did my best to create something that could be shown there, and I hope one day it will be.

Rosie's painful awkwardness, insecurity and, I guess we can call it, culture shock, upon arriving at the poetry festival reminded me a lot of my first animation festival experiences. I suspect you drew on your experiences travelling to film and animation festivals.

Yes, the poetry festival is perhaps the most autobiographical part of the film. It really stands in for the film festivals I've travelled and presented my works in. International festivals are these beautiful oases where people of all different backgrounds and languages and cultures get together to talk about art, our different experiences and viewpoints and about how we get along in the world. It's a great honour and an immensely confusing experience I mean that in a good way... you always learn something that shakes up your worldview, if you are open to it.

Was this always planned as a feature? Did you seek out producers before deciding on the crowdfunding route?

This was always supposed to be a feature. When I moved it to Iran, it was animation that made it possible. I first envisioned it as a very low-budget film and applied to arts councils for funding, but was rejected. Then I applied to Telefilm Canada [Canadian government film funding organization] for development funding on my own. I got executive producers on board to try to push the project forward but prospects of production funding weren't encouraging, especially after the turmoil surrounding the 2009 elections in Iran.

So, I took my storyboard and created a graphic novel, thinking I could get attention for the project that way. But I couldn't find publisher interest. I started to try and build up the story world of *Window Horses* and Stickgirl through different social media sites – Facebook, Tumblr, Twitter, a website, an iPhone app – and finally decided to try crowdfunding and went with Indiegogo because they offered a lot of support.

When did Sandra Oh become part of the project and how involved was she in the story? Was she more a supportive cheerleader or was she active in giving story/character feedback as well?

I called up Sandra – she's an old friend – to ask if she would be the voice of Rosie Ming. She loved the story so much she wanted to become more involved and was the spokesperson for our campaign, basically, and ultimately became an executive producer. Because of her, we were able to attract a lot of fantastic actors who would normally never see this script. Because she had just come off of *Grey's Anatomy*, and there was such a curiosity as to what she was working on now, Sandra got to speak to press all over the world about our quiet themes of diversity, inclusivity, girl power and peace through poetry. It was amazing.

The main character is, as you've deemed her, 'Stickgirl.' This is not her first appearance in your work. Where did she come from?

When I was in my second year of animation at art school I was hit and run over by a couple of cars and was pretty badly injured. I was in a wheelchair for a while and didn't have much energy, a general run-down feeling, you might say. But I so wanted to continue my studies and to make art, so I sat down, one hour a day, and drew my life story, with Stickgirl, who represented all the strength I had in my body at the time. I think that the simplest gestures most clearly show the personality of the artist. We've been together for almost 30 years now, and have made many short films, webisodes and an iPhone app. We've been in doc films, illustrated philosophical texts. *Window Horses* is her first feature role, her first time with a name, the first time she is half Persian and the first time she is voiced by someone other than me... Sandra Oh! She is the kinder, gentler, braver version of myself.

How did [Canadian illustrator and animator] Kevin Langdale become involved and what influenced the design of the film?

Kevin and I have collaborated on many different projects over the years and originally, it was just going to be me and him, me animating Rosie and him animating just about everything else. That's why the design starts so simply. The idea was to have a continuous line drawing in a negative space that got more complex visually as Rosie's world expands. I was influenced, initially, by the animator Paul Fierlinger's simple, continuous line work (and his obsession with dogs, and what that represents) – or my mutated memory of it – when I started thinking of how to make it. I was also inspired by the Japanese prints of the Edo period that are on display at the Los Angeles County Museum of Art that, like Persian miniatures, borrow so much from the style of China's Tang Dynasty. I wanted to reference not just the style, but also a time when cultures borrowed and blended and spoke to each other. One of our early experiments was working with a 3D wireframe model that you can see the vestiges of in the noses of the characters.

You also invited other Canadian animators (Lillian Chan, Shira Avni, Louise Johnson, Jody Kramer) to take on segments in the film.

I always envisioned other artists coming on to represent the different poems and historical sections. This film is from Rosie's point of view and the styles represent her growth and change but also, they show us the power of the artistic process, and the endless possibilities there are to express an idea.

Given the state of the world right now and the apparent tendency towards a sort of right-wing nationalism, this is an especially timely film. It also really captures the often unspoken or undervalued nature of international festivals in that they really are this fantastic place for bringing together people with shared interests from different cultural backgrounds. I think the value of festivals – even with everything being online these days – as an important social and cultural exchange between people of different countries, values, beliefs is hopeful and essential. People still need people.

Yes! Absolutely! That's why I made the film. And it's all about festivals…
film festivals … sharing ideas/values/cultures!

**Has the success of *Window Horses* made it a bit easier to find support
now? Do you have any new projects in the works now?**

Time will tell. I certainly hope so. I hope that I won't have to scratch and
scrape the way I have been. I have several projects I want to pursue. We'll see
what sort of support I can get. The big project is Shanghai Follies, a fictional
tale about my great grandfather who was a world-famous travelling Chinese
vaudevillian acrobat and magician and comic who fell in love with his Austrian
wife, Poldi, in 1908, and toured the world with his mixed-race children and
an amazingly diverse troupe. I've also got a couple of slightly less ambitious
scripts under my sleeve… I only mean that financially. They are all morality
tales of some sort. It's a questioning time in the world.

Elizabeth Hobbs (2016)

16

Elizabeth Hobbs is one of the most imaginative, energetic and perhaps underappreciated indie animators around today. Hobbs' films (including *The Emperor, The Old, Old, Very Old Man, The True Story of Sawney Beane* and *G-Aaah*) are notable for the unusual techniques that range from ink on bathroom tile, typewriters, watercolour on paper, butterfly prints, and rubber stamps. If there is a constant throughout her work, it's the playful proclivity for unusual – yet true – periods in history that touch on witches, vampires, cannibals, Napoleon's penis and a really, really, really, old guy). The blurred, hurried, transient feel of her films aptly reflects the mysterious haziness of her quirky historical subjects, as though we're squinting at faint memories struggling to take shape, find form and become, before vanishing as rapidly as they appeared.

Prior to working in animation, Hobbs made books and prints. "They had little narratives," Hobbs says,

> but I found that I wanted the narrative to unfold in a certain way that couldn't be conveyed on the page, it was about timing and hearing the narrative in a certain voice. So, I contacted a lovely friend called Scott Ward, who helped to find someone to set me up with a camera in a dark room for a couple of days, which led to my first film, a rude film in fuzzy felt.

Happy with the results, Hobbs closed the books and carried on with animation.

While her subjects are rooted in factual historical events, Hobbs's creative process is a bit more freewheeling:

> I never quite know what's going to happen when I sit under the rostrum or start working with my materials, so the work unfolds in the making and there's no compositing or alteration of the work after that, because I like the films to be a true reflection of what I tried to do with the materials. I work very fast, and at the moment I tend to make a little plan, see what happens, re-shoot, see what happened, re-shoot many times, make a rough edit, then re-shoot the whole lot. I hope that the films are as exciting to watch as they are to make.

DOI: 10.1201/9781032683782-16

Yoriko Mizushiri (2016) 17

You don't see a lot of sensuality in animation, especially of the surreal type that involves everyday stuff like snow, futons, and strawberries, but such is the way of the work of Japanese animator, Yoriko Mizushiri. Although she's only made three short films to date (*Futon*, 2012, *Kamakura* 2013, *Maku*, 2014), they've all done well on the festival circuit and solidified Mizushiri as an integral and unique voice in the animation world.

The softness and sensual nature of Mizushiri's work are enhanced by her choice of colours and her emphasis on line movement. "The most important thing in my animation," Mizushiri says,

> is the movement of the line. But I cannot draw too strong a line or the softness will be lost. If you keep your color while consciously seeing a soft thin line properly, you will inevitably have a lot of light colors. Especially thin pink and purple are colors that relate softness and feel of the body to me.

Mizushiri's films capture fragments of life, either in the subconscious or real world. She finds beauty in these overlooked, in-between spaces of life... the small gestures or moments (whether they are in memory, desire or reality) that maybe go unnoticed most of the time (like the beauty of lying in bed or – in this case – a futon, when you're not ready to get up yet and you are half asleep still, and your mind and body drift into memories and sensations).

There is a patient, calm rhythm to Yoriko Mizushiri's films. They are in no hurry to move or even to explain. It's up to the audience to openly engage their senses and feel the film in their own manner. It's a striking contrast to a world very much in a hurry to go somewhere yet, while fecklessly running about, they're actually missing those many, fleeting, beautiful moments that are the essence of existence.

DOI: 10.1201/9781032683782-17

Non-Absorbing? (2017)

18

Indie short animation (not to forget feature) has expanded and matured considerably in the last 25 years or so. Today we are seeing a fairly impressive and diverse tapestry of cultural voices and visions. The heavy and sometimes cornball but earnest symbolism of older voices has been supplanted by films unafraid to tackle deeply personal and relevant social issues (identity, addiction, mental and physical illness, grief, sex, etc.), but has this pendulum swung too far to one side today? Has animation become too insulated, too focused on its own navel now to be of any relevance to anyone? When the general audience looks for answers or perspectives of their society and world (granted, I suspect a majority are understandably just looking to escape the every day), they likely look to documentaries, newspapers, magazines and even live-action films. Animation, for all its maturity and progress, seems to remain largely irrelevant, a cute little niche of artistic expression that languishes somewhere between kids' entertainment, poetry and maybe gallery paintings. In the pre-digital days, animation would have had a tough time being relevant and topical. Technology prevented animators from making work that immediately responded to the shit of the world. That's not the case anymore. There are animators making two, three, or four short films a year now. Given the confusion of the world today and the slant towards right-wing nationalism, should animators perhaps be shifting the focus off themselves and addressing more pressing issues (e.g., racism, sexism, nationalism, technological sickness) or do films that address universal and timeless social issues (like those mentioned at the top) have more of a meaningful impact? Do blatantly political films like, for example, McLaren's *Neighbours* or Priit Pärn's *Breakfast on the Grass* and *Hotel E* or any number of films by Phil Mulloy even have any meaningful impact on audiences?

What do you think?

DOI: 10.1201/9781032683782-18

La Chair de ma Chère (2016)

19

Look, I get exhausted by the plethora of dark, depressing animation at times too, but so be it. Animators and art in general don't owe us a damn thing. It's not mandated to cheer us up or provide an escape hatch or paint the world as it supposedly should be. Art can be a negotiation, a navigation tool designed to help the artist (and ideally the audience) sort through some theme, issue, truth no matter how uncomfortable or painful.

Calvin Antoine Blandin's *La Chair de ma Chère* is one such work that's clearly trying to sort through some painful shit: in this case, a child losing a parent (to suicide, it seems). This haunting psychological thriller looks at loss through the eyes of a child. Unable to process his mother's death – and not receiving much support from his negligent, likely emotionally-stunned father – the boy squeezes himself into a reality where she still safely resides.

Blandin's use of anthropomorphic characters along with the stiff, almost Lego-like environment mirrors the confused and innocent perspective of a damaged suffering child who is just not mentally and emotionally equipped to deal with such a devastating event.

Guided by Blandin's creeping, hesitant camera – that seems to observe through the distant, confused eyes of a ghost – we tentatively traverse vacant stairwells and corridors anxiously in search of a wholeness, a connection that will restore this domestic mausoleum back into a haven of love and comfort.

There are no easy answers to be found here. Even the ending is somewhat ambiguous: has the boy 'awakened' and returned to reality or did he follow his mother's same fateful steps? Nor should there be answers, grief's volume might quieten over time, but it never ever falls silent.

DOI: 10.1201/9781032683782-19

Cheer and Loathing in Animation

20

Of Course You Are (2017)

*People's remarks are so objective, so all-inclusive,
that it is a matter of complete indifference who
expresses them... And so our talk becomes like the
public, a pure abstraction.*
– Soren Kierkegaard, *The Present Age* (1846)

"Of course you are dear," replied every parent to every child after being asked if they were good or smart or talented. Then they grew into animators and still had the same questions. How else can one explain the current obsession with statistics (and yes, we could also include sports and the new analytics regime, but this is an animation site even if I'd rather write about sports sometimes)? Anyhow, here we are. I overheard someone last week humblebragging to some colleagues about how his partner's film had fifty bazillion views because a celebrity happened to retweet it. He was very proud and deeply serious about how important this was. I wondered why though. Now, okay, this obsession with likes/views is merely an extension of getting into a festival competition and/or winning awards. It's also a chance, as a friend told me recently, to impress like-minded executive types who are equally impressed with stats to the degree that they'll offer you commercial work solely because you got picked as a Pimeotube short of the week. I know everyone wants their films

40

DOI: 10.1201/9781032683782-20

to be seen by as many eyes as possible. I'd love it if any of my books became best sellers (hell, I'll be pleased if I ever write one again) or if *Lipsett Diaries* had gotten an Oscar nod, but what does it really mean in the end? You made a work to engage with people, to communicate something to them (at least that's what I assume although some of you just seem to be talking to yourselves). So, isn't the true measure of a work having a dialogue and discussion? Wait… hold on… I went too far… the first measure should be your own satisfaction. For example, I have a couple of books that I am really satisfied with and no amount of lousy sales or poor feedback can ever change that. With them, I achieved what I set out to do. That doesn't mean I'm not listening to criticism or don't appreciate a glowing comment but at the end of the day I've set my own bar and no amount of praise or rejection can really do much to alter that. Second to that is a conversation. I'd find far more meaning in a dialogue/conversation or thoughtful critical review than I would in reading numbers or likes. It's pretty fucking easy to hit the like button and then just turn the work off, but they don't mean much, like a pat on the back maybe. They're hollow and easy. Even comments are rarely more than a few generic congrats or complaints. Rarely do you see truly engaging and thoughtful comments. Okay, so this is nothing new and I certainly like that there are more opportunities for animators now. It's difficult to get into festivals. There's only so much space, so this is a more immediate way of reaching an audience, but a birdie told me that young artists are starting to make films in ways they think will please the Pimeotube curators etc…. (again, nothing new, older animators often confessed to trying to make films that they thought Ottawa or Annecy or festivals in general would accept). To say that this is disturbing and grossly idiotic would be an understatement. Sure, it's scary as shit to be yourself and express what *you* want to say in a way you want to say it. But that's ok, that's how it should be. Otherwise, you're just a generic sheep making the same sheepshit as everyone else (thinking like you) is making. Look, I've seen many of the 'Pimeotube Short' of the weeks and they're not all that great. You gotta remember that human beings are selecting this stuff, not computers. It's a small group of people with select tastes (just like festivals), and to focus all your energies on trying to impress them, to animate for them, well, that's really shortchanging yourself. At the end of the day *you* – not them – are accountable for your life, character and outlook.

On the Other Side of the Woods (2017)

21

The Estonian animation scene, always fascinating and relatively healthy, has nevertheless been criticized for its dearth of female voices. Women were always a part of the animation studios doing both administration and technical/creative work but until recently there were few women directors. That's changed dramatically in the last decade or so with the emergence of talents like Chintis Lundgren, the duo of Girlin Bassovskaja (Jelena Girlin & Mari-Liis Karula), and Anu-Laura Tuttelberg.

Tuttleberg's first professional film, *On the Other Side of the Woods* (2014) is a captivating and curious take on fairy tales, creativity and identity. Fusing live-action, object and clay animation, Tuttleberg explores the usually contrasting worlds of fantasy and reality. But, instead of creating two distinct worlds – as many artists might do – Tuttleberg blends them into a unique black and white world where potted plants sprout into trees, a toppled water bottle becomes a lake, walls become a forest.

"I didn't want to separate the two worlds," says Tuttleberg,

> but to make them fit together instead. I wanted to unify them all into one world and atmosphere. The black and white photography is very graphic and I like that kind of character of a visual, plus I started my studies in art with photography, with black and white analog photography and I find it beautiful and intriguing.

What is equally fascinating is what we don't see on screen. Years pass between the opening and closing sequences. The young artist at the beginning has – it seems – become a mother with a child now. Decay envelopes the space. What has happened in the woman's life? Why is this studio in such a condition? Was this her childhood home or grandmother's house? Was it just forgotten during the natural passing of time? Did she abandon her fairy tale or artistic world for domesticity and the love (e.g., the hunter)?

DOI: 10.1201/9781032683782-21

Near the end of the film, the thread of time snaps, momentarily startling the woman. Something is lost, forgotten during the course of time, but the woman surprises us with a smile, perhaps aware that while the clock has run out on one period of her life, it's in full swing in another, equally fertile period.

The Dark Side of the Toon (2016)

22

Jesus Christ people, I get it! Too many dark weirdo animation films are being created, shown, digested. Been hearing it for years. It's tiresome, people. Films that challenge you are not necessarily dark, weird or what-the-fuck. Maybe you need to be a better fucking viewer 'cause a lot of these films have an abundance of black humour and frequently travel from dark to light. Do you really want hollow unfunny comedies about some 3D animated fuck trying to pop a pimple? Oh, there's plenty like that. You know the ones youngsters make thinking it's gonna get them noticed by a *big* studio.

Some of the best and smartest comedy is dark (see Phil Mulloy, Priit Parn, Joanna Quinn, Michaela Pavlatova, *South Park*). And yes, there are some humourless dark films too (The Brothers Quays, Jerzy Kucia, Piotr Dumala) but what the hell do you want? Find me any animation festival that doesn't have an abundance of overly serious 'oh-so-tragic' poetic 'woe-is-me' wanks? Oh right, you wouldn't know 'cause the ones who complain loudest about the dark films are the ones who don't go to (m)any animation festivals. Look, I don't like humourless films. They're suffocating but at least many of them are somewhat smarter, more mature (okay, that's questionable) than the tripe that says it's comedy.

Besides, it's clearly a reflection of the time. The world is kinda fucked up right now. People are on edge and anxious and distracted and confused and lost. There's the environment, the bombs, threats, economy, cancer, racism, sexism ism ism isms everywhere you look, and that orange guy. Makes sense that animators being, you know, human beings are also affected by this stuff. Hence the bleak anxious befuddling films… they're trying to make sense like the rest of us without coating it in powdered sugar on baked bread with fries (apparently that's a Cuban delicacy).

Better yet, why do you think animation is saturated with strange, mysterious and sombre work? Instead of me having to ask you tiresome questions, why don't you ask the artists themselves? Ask them "what's up?"

DOI: 10.1201/9781032683782-22

Even better, ask yourselves.

And yeah... I stole the title for this Friday column from my wife. She said it's okay. Really. Beats Pimp, right? It's kind of a fusion of Kierkegaard, Hunter Thompson and The Beach Boys.

Daisy Jacob's *The Full Story* (2017)

23

I can vividly remember the last moments of the last day at my grandparent's home. Our family was there. It was empty. No one spoke. We were all looking through the vacated rooms and the blank walls towards times, places, and people long gone. The house was empty, yet still carried the spots, streaks, stains and stenches of the past.

In *The Full Story* (produced by Elliot Tagg and Geoff Morgan), Daisy Jacobs and Chris Wilder's powerful follow-up to their multi-award winning (including a BAFTA win and an Oscar nomination) student film, *The Bigger Picture* (2014), a vacated family home triggers an assortment of painful memories for a man (Toby) as he remembers the effects of his parent's divorce on his past and present.

Now, if one were to think that the success of *The Bigger Picture* would ensure Jacobs an easy time producing and funding her next film, they'd be wrong. While the prize money and crowdfunding (along with funding from Creative England) helped, Jacobs no longer had the technical and creative luxuries of the National Film and Television School (NFTS) to rely upon.

> It was much, much harder to make *The Full Story* as it is far more complex in every way, and that includes logistics and finance. For example, at the NFTS, we were given a large, fully-equipped studio for six months; this time we had to *make* one ourselves in an empty ship-building shed on a former naval base. We did it entirely from scratch, right from blacking out (massive windows!) and putting in the lighting rig. The creative demands alone were punishing. Chris and I animated everything ourselves without any help and I also painted all the sets myself while Chris made all the props himself with only one assistant.

In *The Bigger Picture*, Jacobs and Wilder utilized an impressive hybrid of life-size wall paintings and stop-motion. For *The Full Story*, Jacobs adds real actors to the mix.

DOI: 10.1201/9781032683782-23

I liked the challenge of blending people visually into an animated world. We used live actors primarily to suggest that Toby's memories are vividly real to him. In terms of mood, I think it also contributes a sense of unease, and practically it creates more depth. It means we can exploit the full space for animation and are no longer just working on the walls. I also liked the idea of having no rules and creating something different.

Working with actors – especially children – also created new challenges. "I will never write anything with children in it again. Never," says Jacobs.

All the children that came in cried. At one point, mid-shot, a child smeared paint all over his face, hair and clothes, screaming "I'm green!" I have absolutely no idea why I didn't realize children might be a challenge. I just assumed they would be like mini adults but they are not. They are mad little things and live in a different world from us.

Jacobs was initially attracted to the life-size technique because it liberated her creatively.

"When you make something in a 3D space," she notes,

there is an added layer of cinematography which brings atmosphere to the storytelling. Working life-size also allows me to use large and expressive brush strokes and so 'become' the characters far more intensely——when I draw or paint a character, I do actually become them in that moment. I work well standing up, using my whole physicality to act out what I'm painting, gesticulating and pulling peculiar faces.

In both *Bigger Picture* and *Full Story*, Jacobs deals with painful and confusing events that most of us, unfortunately, have had a taste of. While Jacobs draws on personal experiences, her aim is to make films for other people:

I want to share difficult events with a wide audience in order to present a (hopefully) cathartic and uplifting experience. In this film, the idea of letting go despite past traumas is meant to inspire people to live their lives to the full and not be burdened by the past.

A lot of talented animators have produced amazing student work and then just vanished, some getting lured in by the steadier commercial studio paychecks. Given the painstaking work along with the headaches of financing, I wonder what drives young artists like Jacobs to take on the challenge: "I can see why you'd not make a second film," admits Jacobs.

Isolation, anxiety, stress and mania often accompany each day. It took us two years, unpaid, isolated, and working to the point of exhaustion, to make this film. I had to leave London, my husband, friends and any sense of reality to move back into my childhood bedroom, working in a blacked-out space that was sweltering in summer and freezing in winter to the point where I had on seven layers and had to put carpet down on the floor where I was animating. I would never have swapped that experience for anything.

Half Smiles of the Decomposed

24

The films of Rao Heidmets (2017)

If Priit Pärn and Mati Kütt are the Lennon and McCartney of a certain generation of Estonian animation, then Rao Heidmets is their George Harrison. Often overshadowed by Pärn's – and to a lesser degree, Kütt's – internationally renowned work, Heidmets has quietly gone about his business putting together an impressive body of films that have explored a variety of intriguing political, societal and domestic issues (ranging from mass media, cloning, genetics, creation, and individual and cultural identity).

Though Heidmets (who joined Estonia's Nukfilm puppet studio in 1982 back when it was still a part of the Soviet state-run Tallinnfilm Studio) works primarily in stop motion, his work has no real distinct visual style the way, say, Pärn's work does). Heidmets has used giant puppets, small puppets, actors, sand, yarn and other assorted objects.

What does link his body of work together is an ongoing fascination with the fragile, thin walls that individuals and societies hoist up around themselves (e.g., television, religion, wealth). The often raw and unpolished look of Heidmet's films along with his occasional fusion of live action and puppet reveal a schizophrenic world that skirts between real and unreal, a world that can barely hold together these questionable and unstable layers.

Throughout his work – from the early classics *Papa Carlo Theatre* and *Noblesse Oblige* (which tackle totalitarian society and class structures,

DOI: 10.1201/9781032683782-24

49

respectively) – through to the magnificent *Pearlman* (which addresses the challenge of a society to maintain cultural purity), *Inherent Obligations* (a prescient work that uses fake news before it was even a thing), *Oracle is Born* (not just a slam on religion but also a commentary about how stuck in patterns and belief systems we become) and the recent *Life Before Life* (what happens when ideas we were always taught were true turn out to be false?), Heidmets seems to want to show us – usually with a healthy dose of absurdist humour – just how tenuous, dubious and fallible these structures are, and that ultimately the line between cultivated and barbaric civilizations is a very slim one.

Heidmets has always been quite modest, casual, and straightforward about his work: "I don't feel that I must say something to the world or that my films are so great that people must hear them," says Heidmets.

> It's not so pressing for me to do things. I enjoy the process of making a film. I like the six-month brain workout… when you must always be thinking. You never know what the results will be because you make changes all the time. Maybe I'll stop after I find my perfect film and move on to something else.

Here's selfishly hoping that Heidmets and perfection never shall meet as we can all benefit from his thoughtful musings about society's often grotesque make-up.

Cheer and Loathing in Animation

25

Taciturn Caves (2017)

> *We are so seduced by the quality of the illusions*
> *created by our digital media that the lives we are*
> *living are almost virtual.*
> Robert Ferguson – *Life Lessons from Kierkegaard*

I'm of two sides about Virtual Reality.

Side 1: I don't give a damn about it. It's ridiculous and pointless. Why are they trying to take us further and further from a truth that we can't ever escape: our end? What would Plato or Kierkegaard for that matter (you'll be hearing a lot this year from that old Danish philosopher – who also happened to inspire the title of this column) have made of Virtual Reality and Oculus Rift or whatever the fuck these blinders are called. It's a given that we've all been lurking in our caves staring at the shadows (you can read all about Plato's Allegory of the Cave in *The Republic*), but now it's like we're all huddled in there with headsets on, shifting and thrashing about like cyborg twit of the year contestants... succumbed so deeply to the digital that we're not even seeing the original shadows of reality anymore. It's a manufactured shadow of the shadows…not even a reflection of the reflections. Today's variation of bread and circuses is so layered now that we can't even be accused of living in the past or future anymore cause most of us are swimming through timeless fabrications. Past, present and future all weaved together now into

DOI: 10.1201/9781032683782-25

51

a temporal artifice. When will we stop distracting ourselves from the now? What exactly is so wrong with the moment? Is existential boredom the cause of our endless and seemingly exhaustible self-stimulation? Perhaps if we all just shut up for a second and take a deep breath, we might actually be able to see, hear, touch and feel the moment. Maybe then we'd discover our true selves and from there figure out how to think and feel on our own. That would be truly heroic and revolutionary.

Please pause or take a moment to check your email or FB page while I turn the record over.

Side 2:   Wow, that cynical voice is bleak. Jesus man, lighten up. I mean come on. Hasn't humanity *always* been developing distractions?

How is VR any different than the first cave drawings or the invention of the printing press or those dastardly rhetoricians that Socrates despised? Hey, I mean, I don't believe in any gods or afterlife, so why the hell shouldn't we embrace whatever gives us pleasure? What the fuck is wholeness, oneness and a big ol' satori going do for me once I'm dead? Besides, there was a time when musical instruments, the pen, the printing press, the photograph, typewriter etc., were all seen as menacing new distraction devices. Before that people interacted directly. Their musical and storytelling instruments were their voices and hands and feet. Maybe, say, a guitar was the first step towards self-pleasure, it was something you could strum on your own (nudge nudge, wink wink). The printing press eradicated live communal storytelling. The photograph took over from our eyes. The cinema took it further and deeper, creating concrete caves of light and shadows.

All the way through human history we've seemingly been bored and scared shitless of mortality and in response have developed these endless magic shows. And why not? To paraphrase from the final lines of Woody Allen's *Shadows and Fog* (a film about the futility of defeating death), people don't just love illusions, they need them, like they need the air.

Cheer and Loathing in Animation

26

Jargon of Clones (2016)

Each year for a short period of time, I watch a boatload of episodes of animated series for kids. There are occasionally some interesting, refreshing and unique works (*Adventure Time*, *Regular Show* are obvious choices and even Julia Pott's *Summer Camp Island* has potential) but for the most part TV animation (and yeah, it's primarily stuff from North America) all looks sounds and acts the same: *loud*; *obnoxious*; *sarcastic*. Who mandated this? Why do the characters all have to scream at each other? And it's always these buddy films…. two oddball characters (let's say one is Bread and the other is Electric Heater) who have an assortment of equally bizarre friends and they all race around babbling like they're on Ritalin (sorry…it's called Concerta now). It's all happening in a world that has little to no adult guidance. In fact, it's often a world where adults/parents are portrayed as idiots, as people not to be valued or listened to. So, exactly what type of messages are the kiddies getting from this sensory babbling? And sure, hey, I was a kid once and we were scared of adults or resented them. Cartoons offered a brief respite from their dictatorship but there was also a certain degree of respect, at least until we got older and realized that these poor creatures had no idea what they were doing. Most of these shows can't touch the innovation, openness and inclusiveness of say classic shows like *Sesame Street*, *Pee-Wee's Playhouse* (granted, there was a lot of shouting), *Mr. Rogers*, or even *Yo Gabba Gabba*. Even contemporary shows

DOI: 10.1201/9781032683782-26

from Asia and Europe possess a modicum of gentleness, calm and self-respect. We've become so saturated with sarcasm and cynicism that we're not drowning our kids with it. It's as though we've forgotten what it means to be gentle, to be authentic, to have compassion, to live slowly. I see kids, even my own. They race to finish things, school, dinner, chores. The results range from half-assed to satisfactory. They're all in a hurry but where? Don't we need to remind them to slow down (physically and verbally)...you know just take a deep breath and let life in to settle a bit. 'Cause believe me, once those kid years are over, you're gonna be desperate for everything to slow down a whole hell of a lot.

Cheer and Loathing in Animation

27

Other Dogs Remain (2017)

> Cry 'Havoc!', and let slip the dogs of war.
> William
> Shakespeare – *Julius Caesar*

> *The dogs of war don't negotiate*
> *The dogs of war won't capitulate,*
> *They will take and you will give,*
> *And you must die so that they may live*
> *You can knock at any door,*
> *But wherever you go, you know they've been there before*
> *Well winners can lose and things can get strained*
> *But whatever you change, you know the dogs remain.*
>
> *Dogs of War* – Pink Floyd

A few weeks back, I was writing about the tedium that is cats and animation. Today, at the request of my friend Pookie the Pug, I want to address another injustice in animation: the inhumane disregard for dogs in animation. You see, Pookie is fed up. He says that every animation he watches seems to portray dogs "in an unfavourable light." "Dogs," says Pookie, "get very little love in

DOI: 10.1201/9781032683782-27

animation. They're (he pauses for a moment as a squirrel runs by the window) either unstable idiots (Droopy, Warner Bros' Chester and Spike, Scooby-Do, Disney's Goofy, Ren (*Ren and Stimpy*), Bill Plympton's dogs, Brian from *Family Guy*), colonizers (Joanna Quinn's *Brittania*) victims of human and monkey abuse (Suzie Templeton's *Dog*, Riho Unt's *The Master*) or just outright malignant beasts (*Lupus, Peripheria*)."

From Plutarch to Shakespeare to Pink Floyd (*Dogs* and *Dogs of War*) to Stephen King (*Cujo*), culture has tended to portray dogs as vicious, perverted (AC/DC's *Givin' the Dog a Bone*), violent evil creatures hell-bent on tasting human blood (from Shakespeare to Cujo), dogs seem to be unfairly assigned a masculine trait, or at least a trait that designates violence, menace, bully-ing. Any dogs who are portrayed favourably (Lassie, Ol' Yeller) are frequently punished in the end.

Only a few animation films, according to Pookie, "get it right" by cel-ebrating the tender, loyal, loving and cerebral side of the dog. In Nick Park's *Wallace and Gromit* films, Gromit the dog is clearly the superior being. Charles Schultz's Snoopy, while delusional and possibly insane, has insights into the world his human chums lack. Linus and Charlie and Lucy talk, bicker and ponder, while Snoopy just gets out there and lives. Pookie also mentions Janet Perlman's *Monsieur Pug* as a favourite for its valiant attempt to get inside the mind of a dog. "She really tries to understand the way we see and process the world," says Pookie.

For Pookie, though, his favourite film remains Paul and Sandra Fierlinger's beautiful doggie ode, *Still Life with Animated Dogs* (2001). He feels that "it's the most honest, loving and revealing portrait of dogs and their complex rela-tionship with human beings." While Pookie feels it "sometimes slips into cheesy cliché," he is willing to overlook that because of "the filmmaker's genu-ine love and understanding the essential nature of dogs."

As we continue to walk, Pookie pauses. As he lifts his leg to mark a nearby push, he thanks me for writing this and hopes that this article "will increase awareness and lead to more accurate portraits of our species and a better understanding between human and..."

Before he can finish his heart-wrenching appeal, Pookie races off after a leaf.

Cheer and Loathing in Animation

28

When Machines Attack (2017)

The public is a monstrous nothing.
– Someone.

Once upon a time, a producer called me. His film had been selected for a non-competition showcase in Ottawa. This did not please him. I calmly, and likely nervously, explained my reasoning. There was a pause. He spoke but did not address my explanation. Instead, his only response was that the film had won a grand prize at another big animation festival along with an Academy Award. That, he felt, should be enough to merit the film's inclusion in our competition. I disagreed. Should a festival be selecting (or rejecting) films simply because they were awarded elsewhere? Is that what should really motivate and concern a film festival? Do festivals feel pressured or obligated to show films solely because they won awards or travelled the festival circuit?

If it is, well, it's dishonest and somewhat icky overall because it means that as a curator/programmer, you are not making a passionate and engaged decision. And if you're not doing that, well, what's the point? Why are you even doing this work?

Did the programmer perhaps dislike the work, but then, feeling perhaps insecure, decide that he/she/they might be missing something and so they roll the dice and accept the film anyway? Is it stemming from a worry that they

DOI: 10.1201/9781032683782-28

risk being considered stupid for not seeing what an obviously brilliant film this was?

At the other extreme, there are festivals that won't screen a film in competition solely because it has won many awards or been at numerous festivals. Is this an attempt to carve out an identity for a fledgling festival? Perhaps and I can understand to a degree, but regardless, it again strikes me as dishonest and even a bit patronizing. It's like enforcing a salary cap on animators, punishing them for being successful. And that's wrong. It's dishonest to your audience, the filmmakers and yourself.

Passionately and honestly liking/disliking a film is far more laudable than passively accepting/rejecting it.

It's like so many of us are afraid to be wrong, afraid to put ourselves on the line, afraid to be humans.

Cheer and Loathing in Animation
The Power of Pärn (2016)

29

For years I've endured your jokes, complaints, rants, insults, tweets, letters, rocks, brooms, pucks, wheat, carrots, cows, and buttons about Estonian animation led by the work of Priit Pärn.

> "They're weird."
> "Why are you obsessed?"
> "I don't get it."
> "I want to cry."
> "Fake surrealism." (Is that even possible?)
> "Jury is fixed."
> "It's sexist."

Yet, aside from say Pixar and Miyazaki, has there been a bigger influence on contemporary animation than Pärn? From Igor Kovalyov to *Superjail!*, Pärn's impact has been vast.

Igor Kovaylov was one of the earliest admirers of Pärn. Oh, if I could get ahold of Kovalyov's pre-Pärn art, you'd see just how strong the early influence was. And like the more successful of Pärn's paraders (if that's not a word, it should be), Kovalyov took pinches of Pärn but only to complement and develop his own voice. That voice ended up in the USA in the 1990s and you can see the whispers of Pärn in TV shows that Kovalyov worked on, most obviously *The Rugrats* and *Aaahh!!! Real Monsters*.

In the late 1990s/early 2000s, a trio of young Estonians (Ulo Pikkov, Priit Tender, Kaspar Jancis) carried on the Pärn influence. Jancis and Pikkov studied with Pärn at the Turku Arts Academy while Tender learned on the job over at Tallinn's Joonisfilm studio. Again, while their early films are drenched with Pärn's influence, all three grew and developed their own unique and strong voices.

Around the same time, a young Rhode Island School of Design student had seen some Estonian work at the Ottawa International Animation Festival and what he saw influenced his own witty graduate film, *Mr. Smile* (1999). You can even see hints of the influence in Krause's acclaimed comic collection, *Deep Dark Fears*.

Krause wasn't the only RISD student to feel the power of Pärn. Jesse Schmal's graduate film, *Sub* (2000) and Christy Karacas's *Spacewar* (1997). And of course, Karacas carried that influence (one he's acknowledged) with him when he went on to create the cult TV show, *Superjail!* (the first season of the show was produced by another Estonian admirer, the American animator, Aaron Augenblick).

Japanese animation legend, Koji Yamamura has never hidden his admiration of Pärn. You can see tinges of Estonia in Yamamura's films, *Your Choice* (1999), *Mt. Head* (2002) and *Country Doctor* (2007). Yamamura has carried that influence into the Toyko Arts Academy and even younger Japanese animators like Atsushi Wada and Kei Oyama – among others – have some Estonian vibe.

Most recently, works by Marta Pajek (*Impossible Figures and Other Stories II*, 2016) and Sarina Nihei (*Small People with Hats*, 2015) have carried the Pärn torch.

What is it about Pärn's work (which itself is influenced by an assortment of stuff ranging from Pop Art, Monty Python, Surrealism and George Grosz, to *The Master and Margarita*, *Yellow Submarine* and animation shorts like *Satiemania*, 1978) that continues to appeal to animators?

I think there's probably a bit of that Punk/DIY influence. Pärn's deceptively crude drawings and his non-linear storytelling are universes from the polished and precise works of, say, Disney and the National Film Board of Canada. There is something liberating about Pärn's work that's maybe akin to how people felt when they first heard *The Ramones*, *The Jam* or *The Clash* whose short potent riffs and rebellious demeanour vibrated a sense of hope and purpose for a generation of lost adolescents. That might seem like a strange comparison, but remember Pärn's the guy who made potent anti-establishment films *Breakfast in The Grass* (1988) and *Hotel E* (1992) during when Estonia was part of the Soviet Union. Those films alone were far more meaningful and badass than *Never Mind the Bollocks or Rocket to Russia*. And when you think of Pärn in that context, it's not a stretch to see why so many animators continued to be impacted by his work.

Cheer and Loathing in Animation

30

Mix up the Satellites (2017)

> *I think sequencing is a very important aspect of making a record. It's the same as telling a story or making a film. You want to start strong and end strong with no filler, and if you do have filler, it should at least be an interesting "set up" song— something that makes the next song sound really good when it comes in. It's a little like making out a baseball lineup: The leadoff hitter gets a hit. The second one moves it to first and third, and the third or fourth one brings 'em all in. At the end you bring in your closer.*
> – Robert Pollard

In my biased mind, one of the most unappreciated and overlooked aspects of a festival is the ordering or curating or choreography of a screening. I certainly won't speak for other festivals, but I see it as the most exciting, fun, and important part of being an Artistic Director or Programmer.

I spend 3–4 days shifting and shuffling index cards that I've taped on the walls of our home with the names of each competition film. I don't stop until I feel content with the construction of each of the five short competition screenings (my colleague, Keltie handles all the Panorama programmes). In some

DOI: 10.1201/9781032683782-30

ways, it's like making a film, but it's probably more accurate to compare it to making a mixtape (or an iPod playlist for you digitally-reared kids).

In general, I try to avoid finding themes. Though some years I have resorted to that approach when there's just been such an obvious and weird thematic connection. One year, we had an abundance of films that seemed to chart various stages of life from birth to death. Incredibly, the death films were far cheerier than the birth/youth ones, instead favouring an internal rhythm. It's very musical for the most part. I'll listen to the end credits sometimes or last images just to feel the sound and that will help me lead into the next film.

We also don't finalize the competition list until this sequencing is done, largely because if I find that a film just isn't fitting in with the vibe of the program, well, I'll swap it out for something that does.

Sometimes I'll also place films together that have opposing emotions just to toy with the audience. It's a fascinating social experiment to show a really sad film and then follow it up with something gut-bustlingly funny, or to put a strange Estonian film right in front of the latest Wallace and Gromit.

Unfortunately, sequencing seems to be less of a priority for some Festival Directors who prefer – it seems – to lump works together based on nationality or technique or, more often, the roll of the dice. I've seen so many weak screenings (and probably constructed a few myself) that could have been more bearable and interesting had the sequencing been thought out more.

Maybe it doesn't matter. Most (not all) audiences don't even seem all that aware or interested in such things.

Too bad for them.

Cheer and Loathing in Animation

31

Some Things Are Big (And Some Things Are Small) (2017)

You're sitting in a festival screening of short films. As you scour your festival guide for information about each film, you suddenly pause with dread. Your eyes widen, your heart flutters, your shoulders tighten, while psycho butterflies kamikaze your insides. You gently shut your eyes in the faint hope that calm will once again envelope you. It's too late though. You know this. Resigned, you inhale a long, slow breath and prepare for the inevitable horror: a 20-minute short film.

I suspect we all do it. I know I do.

I'm reading this book called *The Shallows* by Nicholas Carr. In it, Carr discusses how our brains and the way we think and process information is being altered by the internet. In one part he talks about the challenge he has reading books, how he used to easily get absorbed by one but now finds himself restless and distracted after a couple of pages. I feel the same way, and have about a dozen half- or quarter-read books on my bedside table to prove it. Anyway, for whatever reason – probably because I was getting restless while reading Carr's book – it got me thinking about how impatient we are with longer short films (ironic, given the rise of animated feature films). Of course,

DOI: 10.1201/9781032683782-31

I don't think we can fault the internet for this. Animation audiences, juries and selection committees were groaning about these films before the digital age emerged.

Why are we so impatient with and unfair to long short films? These films are usually stuck at the beginning or end of a screening which audiences see as their cue to arrive late or leave early. As festival programmers, we seem to demand more. If you're going to make a long short film, well, it better be a masterwork. Otherwise, why show one good 20-minute film when you can cram three good shorter films into the same space?

Is it merely a symptom of watching multiple short films in a single 70–80 minutes (which is the maximum any decent film curator should force an audience to endure). Maybe it's like snacking all day and then come mealtime, you're not really all that hungry. Sure these short films are temporally brief, but processing and digesting them is quite a meal and before one has ended, before you have time to breathe and contemplate, you're hit with the next short. Actually, you'd think longer shorts would be more welcome cause you get time to absorb it, or sleep to prepare for the next film.

Is this fair? Is jamming a few shorter films better? Is it done to boost festival screening statistics? Is it too much to ask that we give someone 20 minutes of our attention? Most of us happily drift on the internet for 20 minutes or watch a TV sitcom (22 minutes) without much complaint or burden. Why can't we give a long short filmmaker the same attention and patience?

Edmunds Jansons

32

The Wondering Wanderer (2019)

Latvian animator and illustrator, Edmunds Jansons, is one of the few independent animators who seems to thrive on making films for younger audiences. It's a good thing too. These days, much of the so-called children's animation is a garbage dump littered with unimaginative and obnoxious works created in boardrooms by adults who either lost sight of – or never tasted – the joys, freedoms and fears of childhood.

"Quality children's culture," says Jansons,

> is an important part of our society. It's not enough to just import some nice content from abroad. We should communicate esthetical and ethical values from the places where we are from. I don't see many people creating those kinds of works, so I decided to try this myself.

Loosely inspired by mid-20th century children's films and books (notably UPA, the Golden Books series, and authors like Ludwig Bemelans), Janson's works (e.g., *Pigtail and Mr. Sleeplessness*, *International Father's Day*, and *Choir Tour*) are beautifully designed and carefully crafted modern stories (often about children struggling to connect with their parents) that create warm worlds where young audiences are free to wonder as they wander through a world that is mesmerizing, amusing, confusing, and inspiring.

"The style and look of the films is something unconscious," says Jansons. "I grew up with these 20th-century books and films and for me, this aesthetic

DOI: 10.1201/9781032683782-32

builds a feeling of safeness. And that is something I want to share with younger audiences."

Jansons' films are vibrant and refreshing celebrations of the remarkable imaginations and curiosity of children as they roam about trying to carve out a voice and space in a world of distracted and mysterious adults.

Reruns
The Final
Chapter of Rosto's
Dreamworld (2019)

33

Reruns, by Dutch filmmaker and animator Rosto, concludes a tetralogy of films (with *No Place Like Home, Lonely Bones, Splintertime*) that follow members of a rock band, Thee Wreckers, wandering through a rather nightmarish dreamscape that seems to land somewhere between purgatory and hell. Fusing live action, animation, and music (each film is based on a song from Rosto's former band, Thee Wreckers), Rosto creates a blurred and haunting vision that skitters and skulks between the conscious and subconscious.

With the fates of the four band members seemingly settled in *Splintertime* (2015), *Reruns* takes up the story of Virgil Horn (whose head – which bid adieu to its body in *Lonely Bones* – has been carried around by the band) at different stages of his life: child, adult, old man and, yes, skeleton). Arguably more autobiographical than the previous films (Virgil bears a striking resemblance to his creator, Rosto), *Reruns* explores the rubbery border between dreams and memories (themselves dreamy, or as Rosto says, "corrupt" fictions) as Rosto takes us on a tour of his reimagined past. The result is an emotionally charged exploration of the complexity, potency, and ultimate unreliability of both our memories and dreams.

Rosto and I recently had a discussion via email about some of the challenges, pleasures, and themes of *Reruns* and the tetralogy as a whole.

Chris Robinson: *Reruns* strikes me as the most personal of the four films, inspired by a cloudy fusion of dreams and memories…

DOI: 10.1201/9781032683782-33

Rosto: Everything in *Reruns* is real. It's entirely inspired by my dreams and memories. I've had this dream city since I was very young. It has assorted places like my old high school, art school, my studio, and my grandmother's house. The city keeps growing. I could almost make a map of the space. There's also this end-of-the-world part, a big ring road that goes around the city. There's nothing beyond it and it's really not a very good place.

As visually striking as *Reruns* is, the sound seems to carry equal if not more importance throughout.

Rosto: As much as my intent was to build this dreamworld and invite the audience inside, it's not really possible given the various constraints. In the end, it's still 2D, it's a screen. It's not VR, but the sound can bring you, can surround you, and make it a more immersive experience.

Was each film based on a pre-existing song? If so, can you talk a bit about that process of translating a song into a film. And out of curiosity, did you use the original recordings or did you go back and re-record any of the songs, and if so, did the films then change the songs in any way?

Rosto: A beautiful process. I love it, because we're going back to pure intuitive filmmaking here. All the elements of the music are there for me to use (or not), so it's a real luxurious position to be in. (I often realize this when I see a non-musician struggling with getting their film together. It's best compared with making a new symphony with elements of sound, story, picture, music, mood etc.)

Simplest example always is: If you already have a 'lead' in the image, you usually don't need a 'lead' in your soundtrack (usually the vocals of the song), so you get rid of one in your new composition.

There's a lot of 'feeling' and dreaming during this process (like with writing a song, this is not a very 'brainy' process), which makes it so wonderfully gut-oriented. Most of the time, it's about stripping. Killing your darlings. Losing tracks. But for *Lonely Bones* and *Splintertime* I actually had to go back to the recording studio to record new tracks for the new film arrangements. This didn't change the songs anymore (as the earlier films *have* done) since the album's songs were practically all laid down by now.

Water has a strong presence throughout the film, it really enhances this experience of roaming through someone's subconscious and there's the feeling of gasping for air, of struggling to breathe and to stay alive. In fact, that's the general feeling you get with all four films.

Rosto: Water represents the past. The deeper you go, the further into the
           past you travel.

**There's a striking and haunting scene early on in *Reruns* where we see
the young Virgil (and also a young Rosto) roaming around an old house.
It combines actual old home footage, but with effects added (it's a nice
touch that your daughter, Rosie, also portrays the character in some
scenes). At one point, it's almost like the footage is projected on various walls of an old house, which nicely touches upon that idea of these
memories we ourselves project onto spaces. I can remember when our
family was preparing to sell my grandparent's home. I'd spent many
happy times there and the last days in the emptied house were quite
emotional. During those last hours, I'd find myself staring at blank
walls and empty space while being transported back the past through
an assortment of vivid memories (likely distorted over the years) from
my childhood.**

Rosto: My father took this Super 8 footage in 1974 in my grandmother's
           house. I was five years old. Her house was an important location
           and I wanted to portray it. I used this stitching technique to mix
           together some of the old footage. It was like washing a black win-
           dow… and then slowly the room appeared. The technique also cre-
           ated these echoes which complemented the idea of people slowly
           vanishing. The room still exists but unfortunately, some of the peo-
           ple do not anymore.

Did you always envision a quartet of films?

Rosto: It was never about 'story' as much as it was about creating my own
           platform for my own tunes, creating my own *Fantasia*, I guess. As
           soon as I finished *No Place Like Home,* I knew that I wanted/had
           to do three more. Everything in rock 'n' roll comes in four. The 4/4
           beat. The Beatles. Thee Wreckers.

**How much of the final work altered from your original vision? These
appear to be quite challenging and complex films, both technically and
conceptually, so I wonder if technical limitations ever forced you to change
plans.**

Rosto: No, there was no masterplan, no concept, except for the total num-
           ber. The 'rules' of the tetralogy were that the next film picked up
           where the previous one had stopped, that it was musically based
           on a Wreckers song and it had the characters of the Wreckers
           (somewhere).

These films are super complex to pull off and I sometimes feel a bit frustrated that my guys (my team, who were often *so* innovative over the years) never really got the credits, except for a 'Visionary Award' for the unfinished tetralogy at the Sapporo Festival in Japan. I'm mentioning this especially because this *Star Wars* post-guy in that jury recognized it exactly when he said: "We have been developing all these wonderful tools and all we do is make robot films with it. These guys (read: my guys) turned everything upside down and got excited with what *else* you can do with it." Audiences just never 'recognized' the qualities, because it's all done in a computer, innit? And nowadays we 'have an app for that.'

NFB's Montreal Studio Remembered

34

Filmmakers And Studio Employees on Building's Legacy (2019)

In September 2019 (though, given the many delays thus far, that's just a rough guess at the moving date), the National Film Board of Canada (NFB) will bid 'adieu' to their infamous old headquarters after 63 years and say 'bonjour' to a brand new space in the lively Quartier des Spectacles area of downtown Montreal.

Over the years, the NFB's old building has been described as – take your pick – a rundown hospital, a mental institution, an abandoned factory, or adult high school. Those descriptions, born from seeds of loving nostalgia and bitter frustration, reflect the various highs and lows of a globally respected film studio that has endured and thrived in spite of decades of meddling-hand stains left by bureaucratic and administrative vandals.

The old building at 3155 Cote de Liesse (technically in Saint-Laurent, Quebec, just north of Montreal central) right by the highway to Ottawa and near an assortment of car lots, has seen it all (sadly, no one will go on record with the long list of 'nudge nudge wink wink' tales), yet there is one constant. Since 1956, when the NFB moved from its original headquarters in Ottawa, it has continued – despite massive cuts, questionable restructuring,

DOI: 10.1201/9781032683782-34

and iffy leadership – to create some of the most beautiful, groundbreaking, and acclaimed films (animation and documentary) in the world.

As the NFB gets set to move to some shiny new digs, I asked some NFB veterans to share some of their funniest, fondest and not-so-fondest memories of the old building.

PIERRE HÉBERT (FORMER NFB ANIMATOR/PRODUCER/ EXECUTIVE PRODUCER)

The most unexpected and funny thing I can say is that I will certainly miss the British colonial architecture style of the building. I always felt it some-how looked like a British colonial administrative building in the Bahamas, for example. It is not startling architecture, but every morning when I was going to work, it made me think of the Bahamas, where I have never been! I will also miss the memory of Norman McLaren's original studio which disappeared a long time ago. Every time I was walking there, behind the sound studios, I could remember and see the two rather small rooms where Norman and Evelyn Lambart were working.

MARCY PAGE (FORMER NFB PRODUCER, *RYAN*, *THE DANISH POET*, *SETH'S DOMINION*)

It was always astonishing to me that so many groundbreaking and beauti-ful films could come out of such an ugly, prosaic building...but I somehow admired that lack of pretension.

Coming from California, it was like visiting ILM (Industrial Light & Magic) hiding behind a fake industrial storefront in San Rafael. You had to know what went on inside behind the trick appearance. The NFB building I first encountered in the late eighties was a rambling complex with enough ren-ovations and layers of history that there were areas that you might never see, or might discover like in one of those dreams when in a familiar childhood home, a sudden basement or hidden wing appears that you never knew was there.

I came to the NFB just in time to be able to discover a shooting stage not yet completely privatized, filled at one moment with a giant pirate ship (was it for Roger Cantin's *Matusalem*?), and I recall scrounging in the costume department racks for a Halloween party and trekking across the "bridge of sighs" to the abandoned and derelict administration building and imagining a time when that too was bustling with people, or more recently slipping down to the basement with its maze of overhead pipes, lit only with emergency lights and feeling like something out of *The Shining.*

I was, and still am, in awe of the creators who walked those NFB halls and loved to see the threads of history in the leftover artefacts: an animation stand on which Caroline Leaf worked, a pair of slippers worn by Norman McLaren, and bits of film footage tests shot by Sidney Goldsmith for the film *Universe* thrown into a garbage bin, or a file folder filled with reams of John Weldon cartoons, or notes and posters taped to the walls, thinly veiled chronicles of an animator's daily life, or the thousands and thousands of drawings and cels and props and stray bits of animation sets fighting for space in storage. What will we miss? Lots of history in the feel of real things.

What we won't miss is location, location, location, long to reach by public transport, in a wasteland of car dealerships, and highway with no pretty cafés to seduce one off to a long lunch. But like the passionate denizen of Nick Park's *Creature Comforts* shouting, "We need *space,*" I wonder how the new NFB will make do with square footage at such a premium. Will creators find themselves sighing for all that old space, those many rooms, nooks, and crannies offering both creative isolation and voluntary commune with other kindred spirits? These days when I pass by that familiar building off the Metropolitan [Autoroute 40] and see the name and logo, my heart still beats a little faster (and not just with residual stress). I know I will be a little sorry to see the logo come down.

PAUL DRIESSEN (DIRECTOR, *ELBOWING, THE WRITER, THREE MISSES, THE END OF THE WORLD IN FOUR SEASONS*)

What I miss about the old building are the early seventies, when a lot of young talent from different parts of the globe were invited to join the Board; the wild parties we had at the French Animation [unit] where I made most of my films (I remember the one with the full bathtub in which people would cuddle up, or where, in turn, we sang songs of our various cultural backgrounds). The English Animation [unit]'s parties were more formal, standing up parties, having a humorous conversation with drinks in your hands.

At that time, the French and English Animation were two separate worlds; they were hardly in touch with each other, and only a very few animators from both sides would sometimes sneak in to check out the other side.

And every Wednesday there were screenings in theater six, of recently made films, live, animation, whatever; everybody welcome, a very nice tradition.

Some animators who lived far from the awkwardly located building would sometimes stay overnight, hiding in their offices, which was against the federal rules. I remember one guy in his pyjamas being led away by one of the guards when I came in one morning.

At an Xmas party in, what we called the New Building, we once had two 'streakers.' I think they were Co Hoedeman and Anthony Kent. Since they were naked I had a hard time recognizing them.

I guess what I miss most are the adventures of my younger years of which I spent many in that building. Like cycling from downtown Montreal to the Film Board in the morning and trying to get back after the first snowstorm had hit the city that day, carrying my bike on my back through the piled-up snow banks.

What I won't miss are the long, long corridors – from the far end someone would approach you and it was hard to get the knack of the right timing to say, "How are you," and "Not too bad" in response.

And boy, it was really an ugly building in an ugly spot.

TORILL KOVE (DIRECTOR, *THE DANISH POET, MY GRANDMOTHER IRONED THE KINGS SHIRTS, ME AND MY MOULTON*)

I will miss:

- The time-warped, un-artsy, unpretentious geekiness of it.
- McLaren's ghost and The history embedded in the walls.
- The cafeteria and its friendly, nurturing people: they're not coming with us, and I will miss them.
- The jaw-clenched camaraderie during the long, freezing waits for the 460 bus in the winter. Sort of.
- My office. It's the only room of my own I've ever had. Sad.

I will not miss:

- The commute and all the things associated with it, including the jaw-clenched camaraderie at the bus stop in winter.
- The coffee machine. It's really awful.

I loved the early 2000s-era when we played volleyball in the parking lot during lunch.

And the pre-digital era when we had rushes. Those were the days.

Sneaking out for a break on the roof.

Or, did you mean that time when I walked into what's-their-names in the Steenbeck room? Unbelievable.

It always seemed like an incredibly lucky break for me that I ended up working there, and I guess I've just always felt a kind of gratitude towards it and the institution it has housed for all these years.

THEODORE USHEV, (DIRECTOR, *LIPSETT DIARIES, BLIND VAYSHA, GLORIA VICTORIA*)

I'll miss the ghosts of the artists, who passed away. The tortured souls of Lipsett, Larkin, and McLaren were coming often to visit us).

I won't miss the ugly, school-like canteen with the awful food served there. If you survived a lunch at the cafeteria, you are ready for the army or a humanitarian mission in Africa. Also, the corridors, reminiscent of a psychiatric clinic.

There are many favourite stories: Arthur Lipsett chain-locking his Steenbeck because he was afraid of getting his ideas stolen. And of course, there are many loves that happened there. I cannot tell them here, 'cause we will fall into 18+ areas.

JANET PERLMAN, OSCAR-NOMINATED ANIMATOR (ANIMATOR/ DIRECTOR, *THE TENDER TALE OF CINDERELLA PENGUIN, WHY ME?*)

I will miss the cafeteria, a place where filmmakers could informally cross paths, exchange ideas, and inspire each other. In the New Building there will be no cafeteria, but there are lots of fast food places. Not at all the same thing!

I may miss privacy and space, I think there will be less of both.

I will not miss the uninspiring location in out-of-the-way Ville St-Laurent. Nestled between two car dealerships on a highway service road. Also, the 20th-century institutional functional architecture.

My fondest memory is the two Bob Ross group painting events which I organized, one in the English animation studio, and one in the French. There were about 12 participants in each, including animators, office staff, producers, including people who have never painted since childhood. There is presently a Bob Ross room in the French studio, displaying the paintings along with the artist's statements. I hope there will be room for such wonderful silliness in the new headquarters.

JACQUES DROUIN (DIRECTOR, *MINDSCAPE, NIGHTANGEL*)

Some of us had noticed a couple of elderly persons having lunch at the cafeteria. We were curious to know who they were. Here is what they said: "We are senior Americans visiting Montreal. From the highway, we recognized the NFB logo on the building and thought: There it is, let's go in!" So for a whole week, they had found their way to the library and entered some screening rooms to watch films. They had the time of their life and nobody bothered them. That may not happen again.

HÉLÈNE TANGUAY (FORMER NFB EMPLOYEE AND LONG-TIME CHAMPION OF INDEPENDENT ANIMATION)

It was my home for 37 years. I miss the people, I miss the ambience. Each corridor had so much meaning… people I worked with every day.

I miss people that came everywhere from the world to meet Norman McLaren and other filmmakers: Louis Malle, Wim Wenders, Leni Riefenstahl, Jean-Luc Godard, Lotte Reiniger, Indira Ghandi, and so many more. An ugly place for some. For me a fantastic place with so many talented artists, technicians, and government employees.

One story that I heard so many times is that, when the building was built, the employees came to work and went directly to their office via the windows [because] it was easier. True or not, I will never know.

During those years, every corridor meant something: French Program, 2nd Floor; English Program, 1st Floor. English and French Animation departments, so far for everybody.

And then there was the 'pool' in the basement. It was really a large basin. The lab was dealing with all kinds of chemicals to develop the films. I think they had a system that went from the second to the first floor. I remember the smells! Probably a bit toxic, but safe. In any case, in case of a major spill, the chemicals would land in that big 'pool,' not on the ground.

Or the rats floating in Windex. I heard that so many times.

I got really lucky to be there, in that ugly building for so many years. It made my life so much richer.

Kirby Atkins on the 20-Year Journey to Bringing *Mosley* to the Big Screen (2019)

35

After 20 years of writing, drawing, voicing, and tweaking, Kirby Atkins' passion project, *Mosley*, opened in New Zealand theaters earlier this month.

Mosley follows a family of four-legged thoriphants (kind of a cross between donkeys and elephants) who live as slaves on a farm run by a sad and bitter farmer named Simon. One night, the thoriphant Mosley and his son, Rue, discover a cave with ancient drawings of what appear to be upright thoriphants. The discovery leads Mosley on a quest to find out what has happened to his ancestors.

Mosley, a New Zealand and China co-production, is an anomaly in the animated feature circuit. There are no annoying songs or blabbering, obnoxious characters. It's a quiet, poignant and dramatic film (with comic moments) that addresses timeless themes of tolerance, family, and the importance of finding your true self.

Chris Robinson recently met up with Kirby Atkins in Montreal to talk about the ups and downs of making a low-budget, CG-animated feature.

Chris Robinson: I cannot imagine working on a project for a few years let alone 20! What was the origin of *Mosley*?

Kirby Atkins: It's crazy. I was directing the *Jimmy Neutron* series for Nickelodeon in Dallas and I also had a career writing scripts. I was

DOI: 10.1201/9781032683782-35

writing a lot of movies that never got made, but I wasn't on spec back then, so I got paid for it all. I had a few stories that I liked so I kept some stuff that I was either going to do right or not at all. *Mosley* was that thing. I started writing *Mosley* after my daughter was born in 1997. Then I was storyboarding and cutting the film together. I just kept going because I was so into what I was making, even though I was also having bad dreams about films like [Richard Williams's] *The Thief and the Cobbler* and all the ways you're not supposed to make a film. You're not supposed to put yourself so much into a personal project, but I couldn't help it.

Mosley started with the end and the whole idea of these Upright characters. Maybe it was echoing Mickey Mouse and Pluto a bit. Why was Pluto the only one on all fours? What tragic thing happened to Pluto that he can't have a mortgage or wear clothes? Yet they're all in the same world… it must have been some devolution… so that turned into what would I do if I was upright and had hands? And then the idea of standing up to be the character you always should be.

I think this idea of standing up and being true to yourself is a pertinent theme in our day and age, and in fact, a timeless and universal idea that anyone can relate to.

That's the great thing about fairy tales and fables. Anyone can read their own story in them. LeVar Burton was into the project at one point and he talked to me about it. He saw the experience of African Americans. You are kings in one world and less than nothing in another. It's about reclaiming yourself and knowing where you came from and what you are.

The character of Rue was voiced by your daughter when she was seven. How did that happen?
By the time my daughter was seven, I was ready to record voices. This is where everything changed. She had been in my office drawing characters with me. She knew everything about this world and would play the Rue character all the time. So, I thought, let's just play the story and I'll record it. And we did and immediately I knew there was juice there.

15 years later (my daughter is 21 now) when we started production in New Zealand, I handed over these original audio performances of my daughter and me. They thought we should re-record it because of the poor quality of the audio, but I thought that's what makes this, because she would just make lines up. She would make up little asides and things like that. It was lovely and unhindered. She wasn't acting, she was playing. If we had gotten a child actor in, it wouldn't have been anything like that. That's when things really started to come together.

How did you end up working in New Zealand?

Initially, I was working with Pres Romanillos. We were going to make the film in Spain, but Pres became ill and passed away after a couple of years. That grounded everything. After he died I just kept working on it, I don't even know how many years. I was writing and animating, freelancing whenever I could, and then this opportunity opened up to make a co-production in New Zealand.

They were looking for scripts. I had storyboarded the whole film. I handed it over and they said, "Yes, when can we start?" I said, "I'm ready to go now," and I brought in some friends like Manuel Aparicio (animator, *Kung Fu Panda*, *Moana*, *Zootopia*) as animation director and Kathy Graves Toon (assistant editor, *Toy Story 4*, *Rio*) as editor. They felt it was the sort of film that they wanted to work on. It wasn't comedy. It was more a dramatic family film, like *Old Yeller* or *The Black Stallion*.

You've directed TV episodes and a short film, but this was your first time directing a feature. What were some of the most unexpected challenges you faced?

I didn't really have anyone to talk to or vent about it with. I just didn't find anyone who had done this before. I don't know of a lot of directors, so I was just making it up as I went along, and doing what I felt worked. I guess that's what they would often tell you to do anyway. It was like crock-pot cooking. I've had this thing cooking forever, so when it was time to go I was amazed at how many answers I had, but it was frightful because you're playing with someone else's money and if you feel their displeasure you wonder, "Am I doing this wrong or do I keep going?" You're ravenous for encouragement. You think you do know, but you don't know, so when you finally show somebody and then you see that it did work...you just think, "Thank god."

How long was the film in production?

It was about three years with Huhu Studios (New Zealand) and about five studios in China. The crew was just fantastic because it was a film they believed in and wanted someone to make.

I did dailies remotely with China via an interpreter. I'd make videos and go through everybody's shots. Some of the animators were 18 years old, some were 60–70-year-olds. Very eclectic. I never knew names, just numbers. But I felt like I got to know them because they were sitting there acting in the camera for me. I got to really love them. They were fantastic artists.

There were things that could have been better, but this was a 20-million-dollar movie. Lighting could have been better, but you forgive all that stuff if you're engaged in the story.

You voiced Mosley, but you landed a trio of interesting New Zealand acting talent: Lucy Lawless (*Xena: Warrior Princess*), John Rhys-Davies (*Raiders of the Lost Ark*), and Rhys Darby (*Flight of the Concords*). How intimidating was that experience?

They wanted an all-Kiwi cast. I thought of *Flight of the Conchords,* and also John [Rhys-Davies] had moved there after *Lord of the Rings.* [John and Rhys] were so opposite, a classically trained actor and a comedian. And it was electric. John and Rhys were just going off of each other. There were moments like when John and I were doing a scene. He's fiddling with his coffee or something, and I'm looking at his hands going, "That's the guy who picked up the *Lost Ark* with Harrison Ford." And here I am sitting in a room acting out an emotional scene with this guy.

How do you feel now that this 20-year journey is at an end of sorts?

My biggest fear is who is going to know it exists. We haven't gone through the PR mill and we missed the Cannes, Annecy, and Ottawa deadlines. Hopefully, if it does well in New Zealand we will move on to Australia.

I am just so thrilled that a bunch of people will be sitting down, watching it. My fear has been that it would get screwed up before it got to an audience or that I just wouldn't finish it. The biggest compromise I had to make was putting the pop song in the trailer, but I can deal with that. I would say that 85–90 per cent of the film is what I always wanted. I'm not creating any new aesthetics here. I'm not creating some new animation. It's just the story. Animation has been a means to an end to tell the story.

The Imprints of Jacques Drouin (2021)

36

The sudden passing of animator Jacques Drouin from a stroke was a shock to many in animation, especially in the halls of the National Film Board of Canada (NFB), where he was an influential and beloved fixture for decades.

"I thought he was eternal," says former NFB colleague Hélène Tanguay.

"He always seemed to me to be forever young," says NFB filmmaker Don McWilliams. "Jacques was a true gentleman with an iron will, as he explored the human condition and advanced the art of the animated film."

Drouin will be remembered throughout the animation community for his mastery of the pinscreen, the device invented by Alexandre Alexeieff and Claire Parker. Drouin's use of the rare tool left us with a unique body of work, including the widely acclaimed *Mindscape* (1976), *Nightangel* (co-directed with Břetislav Pojar, 1986), and his final film *Imprints* (2004).

Drouin was born in Mont-Joli, Quebec in 1943. His journey towards the NFB began when he was a teenager. "My parents moved to Montreal in 1955 and that was about the time the NFB building was in construction," he recalled in January 2021. "We lived in an area where employees of the Film Board were coming from Ottawa to look for new houses to buy. So, I heard about the Film Board quite early."

A few years later, while in his final year at L'École des Beaux-arts de Montréal, Drouin finally entered the freshly painted walls of the new NFB headquarters in the city. "[Animator] Kaj Pindal was giving occasional talks, and because of this we went to the NFB one day to get our paper perforated," he said. "That was the first time I entered the Film Board."

Drouin's interest in animation grew even more during Expo 67, which was held in Montreal. He visited an animation exhibition where he first glimpsed a small prototype of Alexeieff and Parker's pinscreen. "I remember going to see many screenings of animation during the World's Fair. It was fantastic."

In 1968, Drouin headed west to UCLA to study filmmaking. "I only took one animation class there. It was very basic. I wasn't that interested. I learned

DOI: 10.1201/9781032683782-36

to make dope sheets and prepare artwork but my animation knowledge was very limited." Drouin made a few films at UCLA (including the animated short *The Letter*) before graduating.

Back in Montreal, Drouin began work as an editor for TV sports programs. He did this for a couple of years before getting up the nerve to go to the NFB with some animated films he had made. "I had done some pixilation and cutouts and I didn't see much of a future with my job. I was not too happy about the work, so I went to see René Jodoin [head of the NFB's French animation unit]." About a year later Drouin received a call from Jodoin's secretary encouraging him to apply for a three-month internship in the animation department. He went for the interview and was chosen.

During the internship, Drouin stumbled upon a device that would change his life. "I was told that the pinscreen of Alexeieff was there. I got a 16 mm Bolex camera and [filmmaker Norman McLaren] told me I could take a few days to test the pinscreen." Drouin had done some engraving work in school and saw possibilities with the pinscreen. "I thought I was the ideal person to try it. I felt there was a connection since this was the invention of an engraver [Alexeieff]. I was there at a very good moment. It's changed my life."

For the rest of his internship, Drouin experimented with the pinscreen, eventually completing *Three Exercises on Alexeieff's Pinscreen* (1974). After the internship, Drouin went back to editing. It would be a couple more years before he returned to the NFB to pitch *Mindscape,* a pinscreen film about a painter who enters his own painting.

Drouin knew he wanted a film without words that fused the real and the imagined. As he explained:

> I really liked Saul Steinberg drawings. One of them is of an artist with a fingerprint for a head. It struck me that it was about impressions left behind in a painting. I was also interested in Carl Jung at the time. I just put it all on paper and made a few images that became more or less a storyboard. I then figured I had a nine-minute film and it would take me nine months to make it. It ended up taking twice as long. I really had no idea how much time would be needed between each image. I went with intuition and little precision. There was a lot of improvisation that happened.

Mindscape made its debut at the inaugural Ottawa International Animation Festival in 1976, where it took home a jury prize. More importantly, this was also where Drouin met Alexeieff:

> McLaren insisted that Alexeieff come to see *Mindscape* in person. We spoke a few words during lunch. That evening the film was shown and as a gesture of continuation, a 35 mm print was given to him after the screening. Then I visited him in Paris the following year and we had some conversations. I probably saw him three or four times before he died.

Despite the praise for *Mindscape,* Drouin found himself going back to editing work again. "I struggled during those years doing many things," he said. In 1981, he would finally be hired as a full-time director at the NFB, a position he maintained until it was abolished in 2004.

After *Mindscape,* Drouin made *Nightangel,* a story about a blind man and his guardian angel that combines puppet and pinscreen animation (with colour, for the first time in his filmography). This challenging co-production – Czechoslovakia, the partner country, was in the midst of many sociopolitical changes – was co-directed by Czech animator Břetislav Pojar.

Outside of contributions to a handful of animation projects, Drouin would not make another film until *Ex-Child* (1994). Made for the well-intended but poorly conceived *Rights from the Heart* anthology series (which was inspired by the UN Convention on the Rights of the Child), the film tells a story of a father and son who are enlisted to fight in an unnamed war. While there are some striking moments, for the most part *Ex-Child* feels a bit stiff and naïve.

Drouin acknowledged problems with the film but said that it was a learning experience:

> With the limitation of the story, it pushed me to do something other than metamorphosis. I had not really done very realistic actions with the other films, but with this I had to make some people walk. It was a challenge for me to do something that was not too friendly with the pinscreen.

His next film, *A Hunting Lesson* (2001), was based on a famous children's book by Jacques Godbout about a boy who is fascinated by his neighbour, a hunter. Drouin recalled:

> That film is probably the most illustrative I could get with the pinscreen. It was another kind of challenge because I was shooting in color and had to make some ambience with it. The pinscreen was also too small for the images I wanted to do, so I had to make separate sets that I would photograph and make believe it was a continuation of the pinscreen itself. It was fun to try, but I spent too much time trying to solve puzzles.

Imprints, the director's final short, marked a shift back towards a less linear, more abstract approach.

> It was a very physical film. I was sweating all day because I was working under difficult light conditions and making the screen move. I had a device to make it turn. It was like making a first film again. I was over sixty and I guess I finally lost my caution.

Before heading for the NFB exit doors, Drouin made sure to share his knowledge of the pinscreen. Marcel Jean, artistic director of Annecy Festival, remembers: "He gave a masterclass and animator Michèle Lemieux had the opportunity to touch the thorny beast." Lemieux went on to complete her first pinscreen film, *Here and the Great Elsewhere* (2012).

"Jacques gave me so much," she says.

> To start with, the privilege of being his successor to the pinscreen. He gave me room to be myself, along with the confidence to tackle this somewhat terrifying tool. Those hours we spent side by side as he taught me how to repair and maintain the pinscreen are something I will cherish forever. He was passing on the role of protector of an imposing but fragile instrument, one haunted by its inventors' painful past, and I understood that I had become its keeper and curator. These moments are among the most precious, the most moving, of my entire life.

"A few years later," adds Jean, "Lemieux then gave a masterclass to train young French filmmakers on the pinscreen. Today, the pinscreen is alive and well and this is largely indebted to Jacques Drouin."

We can learn much about animation and its expressive reach by revisiting Drouin's career. But at the end of the day, what matters most is the quality of the person behind the works. Drouin was a stellar human being known for his compassion, humour, humanity, and modesty. The disbelief and deep grief that many are feeling over his loss speaks volumes about his character.

"Throughout his career," notes Julie Roy, the NFB's director general of creation and innovation,

> Jacques carried the legacy of this imposing apparatus of film heritage. But he also stood out for his exemplary involvement in the day-to-day activities of the NFB and with the broader animation family on the world film scene. He was endlessly erudite, a patient and attentive teacher, and a warm and caring colleague. But above all, a man of exceptional humanity.

"The single greatest kindness ever offered to me by a work colleague," says Halifax animator Heather Harkins,

> was the moment when Jacques Drouin pulled me aside in the corridors of the NFB in 2003 to ask, "Are you okay? This place is not a normal place." Full disclosure: I was not okay. He was warm, friendly, and always willing to make room for one more person at his cafeteria table. "Day after day, Jacques showed up to work at an institution whose highest executives seemed indifferent to its artists, and he persisted in sharing his bright beautiful creativity with the world."

Raw Power
The Films of Terril Calder (2020)

37

In the realm of independent animation, Métis artist and animator, Terril Calder, has been an influential force since making her first stop-motion films. They have played around the world, winning awards at Sundance and Berlin. The Toronto-based artist's work, which has focused almost exclusively on indigenous themes, has also inspired other First Nations animators including Amanda Strong. Calder's films are raw, unstable and haunting, tackling a number of personal and difficult issues like identity (*Choke, Canned Meat, Vessel*), memory, isolation, and the unspeakable horrors of residential schools (*Snip, Keewaydah*).

A Drawing major graduate of the Fine Arts program at the University of Manitoba, Calder came to animation through Winnipeg's Video Pool Media Arts Centre.

> "Animation," says Calder, held and holds so many possibilities to tell my stories and bring a different perspective to screen to make change. It really is the sum of all of my parts. Activism, Storytelling, Art, Painting, Sewing, Photography, Compositing…it completely challenges me in every way.

After moving to Toronto, Calder learned 3D computer animation. "I thought becoming a CG animator would be a good career choice as a struggling performance artist." Calder found it difficult to find work in the animation industry. "Even though I was at the top of my class, the industry at that time was pretty sexist. An older native woman didn't really fit into the hip work culture that they were trying to cultivate."

In defiance, Calder fused together performance art, storytelling and animation. Her experience with 3D animation convinced her that she needed to work in a manner that was more intimate and physical. "I needed to get my hands dirty," Calder adds.

 DOI: 10.1201/9781032683782-37

My passion is exploring the physicality of the medium in Stop Motion. My first film (*Canned Meat*) went to Rotterdam and I learned so much very quickly about the power of the medium and all of the possibilities. Films get into the dialogue of people often becoming our frame of reference for knowledge and unlike the art I was doing, I didn't have shipping issues... just a link to get it into the world. It's like it has a life of its own. It makes friends and it comes back to you. I was hooked.

After her second film, *Choke*, was recognized at the Sundance Festival, Calder was approached by Dreamworks. She knew this wouldn't be a good fit.

I really began to understand the value of being able to tell my stories my way and I wouldn't change that for anything now. It's okay not to fit in because it forced me to create spaces where I do. I was determined that if I wasn't able to get on the first rung of that corporate ladder that I would build my own and somehow get in closer to the top. Knowing a life with loss makes you brave as though you've nothing to lose.

Calder's recent film, *Meneath* (2021), is a rough, raw, and brutally honest gem that explores, via a little girl, the deeply troubling and divisive experience of growing up split between two cultures, your natural one and your colonized one.

Through Baby Girl, Nokomis, and that Jesus guy (well, this is the fantasy White Jesus – which the film acknowledges and questions – as opposed to the historical flesh and blood dark-skinned fellow who would have been horrified at how his name and skin colour have been appropriated and altered by the Church and their ilk), Calder contrasts the positive, compassionate Seven Sacred Teachings (Love, Respect, Wisdom, Courage, Truth, Honesty, and Humility) with the guilt and shame-based tone of the so-called Seven Deadly Sins (Lust, Gluttony, Greed, Sloth, Wrath, Pride, and Envy).

While this is Calder's own story, it's certainly no stretch to read the film in the context of the atrocious cultural genocide at Canadian residential schools. *Meneath* is a haunting and necessary reminder of the devastating consequences of colonial systems that continue to devour and destroy people every day.

Yet, for all its darkness and bite, *Meneath* is ultimately a story about hope and healing. Strikingly designed and animated, Calder has crafted one of the most disturbing, important, and urgent works on the animation circuit.

Animation needs more films like *Meneath* and more bold voices like Calder's to get us squirming uncomfortably in our cosy seats and towards a place of not just compassion and understanding but meaningful action.

Inspired in part by Calder, there has been a slow, steady rise of animated films created by indigenous artists during the last 10 years or so. There are a variety of reasons behind this rise, some of which overlap with the general rise in animation production. Advancements in technology have made animation a more accessible and affordable process for many. "We grew up in communities that foster creativity and beading one bead at a time is a little like putting together an animation," says Calder.

> Animation is accessible. A free app and a few sheets of paper is all you need to get started. I'm excited to see how animation evolves for the creative young bucks coming up who all have amazing stories to tell. Stories that need to be in the world.

Diggin' them Bones

38

Joaquín Cociña and Cristóbal León Discuss Los Huesos *(2021)*

Los Huesos ('The Bones'), the new short puppet animation film by Chilean directors Joaquín Cociña and Cristóbal León (*The Wolf House*), is billed as a restored version of the first Chilean animation film.

Shot with a 16 mm camera, this faux 'restored' film (executive produced by horror director Ari Aster and made in a year for only US$20,000) tells the story of a young woman who summons the help of spirits to bring two corpses (Diego Portales and Jaime Guzmán) back to life.

Combining dark, absurdist humour with Chilean political history, *Los Huesos* is a piece of creepy magnificence that beautifully captures the look, pace, and tone of early 20th-century animation films while slyly commenting on the socio-political state of contemporary Chile.

Chris Robinson: Which came first: a story or the concept of doing a fake archival film?

Cristóbal León: We never have just one starting point. We have a lot of ideas that we try to connect. Sometimes we forget about one idea, but it's still there, you know. We have very confusing processes.

DOI: 10.1201/9781032683782-38

One of the starting points was that we were in the middle of a social uprising in Chile in 2019. We call it 'Estallido Social' which means social explosion. We inherited the political system of a dictatorship. The gap between poor and rich people is wide. It's a very unfair system. So, this was the context in which we started to think about this production. We took two figures of Chilean history, one from the 19th century and one from the 20th century. They were both defenders of the oligarchy. We wanted to get rid of these leaders somehow and liberate Chile from this oppression. Not that we are taking ourselves so seriously. It's not like we think our film is going to change anything.

Joaquín Cociña: The other context was film history. We need to create a fake creative mind behind the film that is not us. It gives us more freedom and distance. We've also been interested in early cinema. At the beginning of the 20th century, there was this incredible creativity. There was Georges Méliès, a magician making fantasy films; then you had a more documentary-style approach from the Lumière brothers. Two different streams. We're trying to approach projects thinking about those early years. With *Los Huesos*, the idea is very raw. We are pretending we are creating the first animation film. We thought it was funny to imagine that Chile was the birthplace of animation. We then thought of [Ladislas] Starewicz's first films, made using animal and insect corpses. We thought they were beautiful. So, we imagined that we were animating dead bodies in the early 21st century. We found that funny.

Speaking of corpses, non-Chilean audiences (like me) might not know who these two 'corpses' are from the film.

León: Actually, they are copies of our bodies. Joaquín is the guy who wears glasses. The other guy looks a bit like me, so we decided that I'd be that guy.

Joaquín Cociña: Diego Portales was a political figure who was a defender of the oligarchy near the end of the 19th century. He became sort of the hero of the right-wing conservative movement in Chile. He could have been President but wasn't interested.

León: He was a businessman who used politics to make things easier for his businesses. We grew up during the Pinochet dictatorship in the 1970s. In our history books from that time, Portales was praised for bringing order to modern Chile.

Cociña: Jaime Guzmán [the figure with the glasses] was the brains behind the Pinochet dictatorship.

Is Constanza based on a historical figure?

Cociña: She was the mother of the kids of Diego Portales. She was 14 years old when they were having some form of sexual relationship. She had three kids with him. He never married her, which was a bad thing to do at the time. She was sick and locked up all her life. Her children were taken away. The story goes that she never stopped waiting for Portales to marry her.

What's fascinating is that as deeply rooted as *Los Huesos* is within Chilean history, an international audience can still connect to the film on different levels. When I first saw the film, it triggered thoughts about the murders of Indigenous children at these horrible Canadian residential schools.

León: We wanted to make a film that is local but also universal. We designed Constanza with a Chilean Indigenous person in mind because we wanted that extra layer.

On a technical side, you did a remarkable job re-creating this so-called historical film. The lighting, character design, and pacing all bring to mind early animation films.

León: We animate only in camera. We don't use any software. I love that dark room of the camera where you never know how it's going to turn out. A 16 mm camera is radical because you don't know what's going on. We enjoy accidents, bringing mistakes into the process. I enjoyed the mystery of not knowing what would come out of the camera.

Cociña: We also avoided rushing the cuts. In early cinema, the scenes are longer and often go on and on.

What was your approach in terms of music? How did Tim Fain end up part of the production?

Cociña: This was the first time we called a musician. In old films, music was performed live in front of the audience. We wanted to do something based on Chilean musicians of that time. Chilean musicians then were copying European musicians like Chopin. Adam Butterfield [who became executive producer] saw the film and wanted to be involved. He knew Tim Fain and recommended him.

Leon: Our only instruction was that it should be like Chopin but from hell. A very demonic and distorted version of Chopin. At one moment, I had an idea of tuning into a radio that plays stations from other dimensions.

For such a dark film, there is a lot of humor: a painting of you both as cavemen in one scene; visible puppet strings; wrong body parts on the corpses; private parts covered by a glove.

Leon: Almost all of our works begin with jokes. The truth is, I mean this honestly, we always want to do funny things, but the results are always terrifying. We seem to be bad comedians. But we will work on it. We try to have fun working. I am fascinated by artists who manage to combine comedy and horror, like Jordan Peele. I think art is very much about connecting emotions that seem separate.

Let's end with everyone's favourite question: what are you working on now?

Leon: We are working on a movie temporarily called *Los Angeles*, and it will be our first attempt to mix animation and live-action into a feature film. It is a film in which we try to revisit, in our way, the history of fantasy cinema, with its various techniques and aesthetics. We are in the stage of rewriting and searching for co-financing.

The Meaning of Love

39

Making The Windshield Wiper *(2021)*

Love. Has there ever been a more alluring, mystifying, menacing, or misunderstood word? A feeling that has caused more joy, pain, or utter confusion, or led humans to greater heights and deeper falls?

In the short film *The Windshield Wiper*, which debuted at the Cannes Film Festival in July, Alberto Mielgo attempts to uncover what it is about this thing called love that so enraptures humanity. Mielgo – who was art director on *Tron: Uprising*, directed the segment 'The Witness' on *Love, Death & Robots*, and did early production design work on *Spider-Man: Into the Spider-Verse* – held many roles on the short, including director, screenwriter, editor, and sound designer.

Framed by a philosopher in a café overhearing assorted chatter above love, the narrative moves through a series of vignettes related to loves lost, found, and missed. We meet a homeless man who mistakes a shop window mannequin for an old flame; a suicidal woman; a couple sitting silently on a beach; a man and woman in a grocery store, too busy scrolling for love on their phones to recognize that it might be unfolding next to them.

Inspired by observations, encounters, and personal experiences, Mielgo attempts to reveal the impossibility of knowing just what love really means, especially in a world where random in-person encounters have been replaced by technologically mediated swipes and likes.

Combining keyframe-animated CG characters with digitally painted backgrounds, *The Windshield Wiper* is a poignant and visually impressive work that captures the challenges, superficialities, and chances of modern love.

DOI: 10.1201/9781032683782-39

Chris Robinson: What are the origins of *The Windshield Wiper*?
Alberto Mielgo: It's a very personal film, so personal that it's extremely subjective. Like a voyeur, you get a peek at different lives for a minute.
I wanted to show how love from the outside is something we don't
know much about.

I had a few vignettes and was obsessed with love. The philosopher was the first
of my ideas, in fact, and what triggered the main story. I was having lunch in
that same café in Madrid overhearing conversations, and the structure of the
story came fast.

I remember putting together a whole storyboard and saying, "Let's see if I
can direct a film." I started some production with some studios but that didn't
work. Then I realized it had to be done in a very independent way.

How long did it take to settle on the story and characters?
Mielgo: I did it pretty quickly. I did the storyboards over a Christmas holi-
day. I had some characters (all invented, but based on pieces of
myself) and vignettes and personal experiences, and I just started
laying them out and doing the editing. Later, I was adding and
removing scenes. The base was done fairly quickly.

Leo, how did you end up working with Alberto on *The Windshield Wiper*?
Combining keyframe-animated cg characters with digitally painted backgrounds, *The Windshield Wiper* is a poignant and visually impressive work
that captures the challenges, superficialities, and chances of modern love. I
spoke with Mielgo, as well as producer and lead artist Leo Sanchez, via Zoom
to discuss the long process of making the film.
Leo Sanchez: Alberto and I have known each other since back in the day
in London. I arrived in London in 1999 and was there until early
2006, when I moved to L.A. Alberto has a similar trajectory, just
different years. We met there and have remained friends.

Alberto and I were hanging out. He showed me the animatic of his new short
film and I loved it. I offered to bring my studio, and experience in 3D and character creation and development, to the project. So one thing bled into another.
It went from doing service to co-financing, and I was in charge of the front-end
3D pipeline and character creation.

**Alberto, you're coming from a more commercial background. Do you
make these side projects to keep yourself sane or do you see
yourself moving more towards personal projects?**

Mielgo: I've been working in commercials because I need it, but I would love to gravitate towards more personal work otherwise. It's very important to be pure with my art. It happens more and more that big networks approach me with scripts and ideas that do not resonate with me. They're juicy in terms of money, but I refuse to go that way.

I'm humbled that big networks approach me, but then they say they don't want nudity and sex, which is a part of my work. It's a bit offensive because it's like liking a person for how beautiful they are but telling them not to talk.

Talk a bit about the design and overall technical approach
Mielgo: In terms of design, I come from an art direction and painting background. When I'm directing, I like to design the character, design the clothes, the overall look of the film. That's something that obsesses me.

Like 'The Witness,' *The Windshield Wiper* is very simple in terms of technique. The same way that Master Disney was doing it back with *Bambi*. We have a background that's like a 3D painting, and then a character walking around within that space. That's very much what we did here and with 'The Witness,' but instead of having a 2D character, you have a 3D character walking within that space.

Sanchez: On the character side, one of the things I knew looking at Alberto's work: it has very graphic but tangible lighting and texture. That was my perception. One of the things was to work on the rendering and lighting in 3D, but also to get Alberto's graphic level onto the model, the designs, and the animation.

We developed custom tools that allowed us to meticulously sculpt the characters on each shot, so we could get the level of graphism required by Alberto's style and art direction, preserving a much more crafted feel.

Were your roles clearly defined or was there a lot of overlap?
Mielgo: Leo and I have separate studios, but in a way, we were going in the same direction. It was more like two creative forces that needed to be aligned. We've been friends for a long time, so that's overlapping too and Leo has a role as an artist too. There were a lot of moments where we thought this was getting messy. It wasn't a field of flowers. It's not easy to make a film with friends, but the film reflects love.

Sanchez: At the end, we put the credits as we best described. It was Alberto's vision, and I translated his characters from 2D paintings to 3D. It was a great synergy. We've never really worked together so it was quite interesting. Not being a commercial project meant there was room for evolution and change.

How long were you in production and what was the budget?

Mielgo: I would say forever. It's not a financed film. We did it for the sake of art and with no money. We were doing it in the evenings or between jobs. If we got a big gig, we'd have to stop. We might leave the film for a year. So from beginning to end – and there's Covid, which forced us to stop for a year – it was probably six years. It's not firm because we can't quantify it like that.

Sanchez: In terms of budget, it would be so unfair to just throw out a number. There is so much love put in this work, uncountable numbers of hours we have put in all these years, and the work of amazing artists around the globe just with a true passion to be part of this.

Let's talk about love. Are we meant to find true love, to just love one person? Sometimes it feels like love is a brand that's sold to us to rush out and consume.

Mielgo: I am extremely cynical with love. Maybe I can answer best by explaining the title. When it rains while you're driving, the windshield wiper creates a sort of pattern. Each time you clean, the pattern appears again but completely different.

Love is like this. It's always going to change. Maybe it's called 'flove' the next time or 'flaff.' Maybe we struggle so much with love because we try to define it. No one relationship is the same. It's complex and there's the commercial part of love: dinners, proposals, Valentine's, and all this crap.

You've got a segment with two phone-obsessed people in the grocery store completely oblivious to the possible love that is standing right next to them. Do you think technology has made it harder to find love or is it just reflective of what the next generation wants?

Mielgo: I used to be more active to meet people in person. Hollywood films are full of accidental encounters, but nowadays because of technology and changing societal codes, it's maybe made it more difficult to meet people. Yet dating apps are also connecting you with people you might never see in your life, so I have a very mixed feeling about this.

Aside from the time and lack of funding, what was the most challenging part of this long process?

Mielgo: I think Leo or anyone who works in 3D will agree: 3D is the most challenging. It's extremely unexpected. There are a lot of things that can happen and go wrong. Why did the character come out without hair or a head? It's very frustrating. The technical side just exhausts everybody because there's one mistake after another.

Sanchez: Yeah, you tend to underestimate the technological side, and we were doing this on the side. If we had more financing it would have been a different story.

Mielgo: It was nuts.

Just like love.

Animating Anxiety (2021) 40

Anxiety, insecurity, and depression are beasts that many of us know first-hand (especially in the pandemic). But it can be hard to explain precisely what it is that's eating at us. Whether with a therapist or a family doctor, I sometimes get stuck trying to find the appropriate words to describe what I'm feeling. We end up wishing the other person could just jump inside our brain.

Caroline Robert's interactive animated work *Brainstream* lets people do just that, in a sense. Made for the National Film Board of Canada's (NFB) interactive division by Montreal's Studio AATOAA, *Brainstream* presents itself as a (fictional) Health Canada project that allows anyone to get a brain massage by streaming their cerebral activity. In this case, the viewer is invited to massage the brain of a young woman named D.

"When my daughter was born six years ago," says Robert, a visual artist known for designing Arcade Fire covers,

> I was reading a lot about how the brain works in young children. Then I read about the brain in adults, and the way it functions and reacts to different stimuli or emotions. I was really fascinated by the way we can get stuck or it can change and reshape when it learns new things.

Brainstream's animation and design are relatively, and appropriately, straight-forward. Reminiscent in parts of Peter Foldes's classic NFB film *Hunger* (1974), the raw, scribbly look aptly matches the way many people draw (while channelling something of their inner chaos). Viewers – we are led to believe we are among many simultaneous participants – are asked by D to use their computer mouse to massage her.

The massaging triggers different parts of her brain, distorts and generates new images. During the experience (which we choose to participate in for either five or 20 minutes), we see D's memories, from which we learn about her family, friends, and school life, her assorted menial activities (cutting her hair herself, unclogging a toilet, teaching her little sister how farts work), and her demons of shame, guilt, and anxiety.

DOI: 10.1201/9781032683782-40

"I wanted to experiment with 2D animation and create some kind of living matter that could react in real time to touch. We did some experiments like this in past projects for the NFB," says Robert, who frequently collaborates with her AATOAA (and *Brainstream*) colleagues Vincent Morisset and coder Édouard Lanctôt-Benoit. The group previously made the interactive work *Bla Bla* for the NFB. "I also wanted to use animation to morph at any time without a timeline," she adds.

It's a fascinating idea. On the one hand, we learn more about social anxiety, self-loathing, and the unpredictability of the brain. D addresses her issues in a funny, self-deprecating manner that takes the edge off them, for her and us. As viewers, we find comfort in D's openness. She humanizes her experiences, making them relatable, humorous, and fixable.

"I wanted to create characters that were annoying, but that become cute in a way so that we can distance ourselves from them and not take them so seriously," adds Robert. "We can be so intense with ourselves and say things to ourselves that are really mean."

Brainstream is relatable for any age group, but teenagers will no doubt connect strongly. The choice of a teenage female protagonist aptly reflects the prevalence of anxiety among young people growing up in the age of social media and the internet. They are being bombarded with information, images, and constant BS. Many do not yet have the tools to sort the good from the nonsense.

"I have lots of friends with kids who have a lot of anxiety," says Robert. "It wasn't my original intention to make something for young girls or young people in general, but many kids have more anxiety than ever."

Brainstream is also subtly subversive in that it encourages viewers to use their mouse for a purpose with more meaning than scrolling through social media feeds. "We spend so much time and energy just moving our fingers or mouse, and I thought that maybe I could do something to take advantage of this energy, to translate it into something that could help someone," says Robert. "This was the premise of the brain massage idea. A tiny gesture could be gratifying and meaningful in some way. You would be helping someone just by touching your screen."

At times, *Brainstream* feels too facile. Many of the issues it addresses are linked to our society. We are living in a hyper-consumerist, capitalist system that doesn't suit us. The system is making us sick and to understand that, we need to go beyond an individual's brain and explore the social and economic conditions triggering these mental health issues. Granted, that's a big, messy, complicated issue with no overnight cures.

But as viewers, we feel better from listening to D. Hers is like a safe, friendly voice in our head (enhanced by Mathieu Charbonneau's sensitive, almost ASMR-like soundscape). We feel we've helped her, and in doing so we feel a bit better about ourselves.

Brainstream reminds us that human connection – being able to listen and engage with each other – is key to finding some inner harmony. When we see that we're in this shit together, it can make the demons a lot more manageable, and even laughable.

Bob Spit (2022) 41

One of the most refreshing and surprising gems from the animation circuit in 2021, Cesar Cabral's *Bob Spit: We Do Not Like People* is unlike anything usually seen in animation features: an ingenious blend of documentary and clay animation, mixed with a punk, road-movie vibe.

Think of Will Vinton fused with William S. Burroughs, with a dash of *Mad Max* and The Clash, and you get an idea of the film, which won prizes at Annecy and Ottawa.

Bob Spit, which was made for USD$1 million with a crew of about 200, is split into two storylines. In the first, famous Brazilian cartoonist Angeli is interviewed by a camera crew. He speaks of his struggles as an artist and often being stuck with character creations that he's outgrown, notably his punk alter ego, Bob Spit. He's killed off popular characters in the past, and now it's Bob's turn.

The interview scenes are all done with clay animation yet strive for a strange realism and authenticity. We see moments where Angeli just sits between interviews, scrolling on his phone. Occasionally, we see the boom mic in the frame, or the camera simply rests on a shot of an empty chair while Angeli goes out for a cigarette.

In the meantime, in another space – inside Angeli's head? – Bob Spit and other Angeli characters, including a group of murderous beings who look like mini versions of Elton John, get wind of Bob's impending death. He decides he must try to escape from his barren landscape and confront Angeli once and for all.

But is there a creator to find, or just another creation?

Bob Spit is a complex, mind-twirling exploration. On one hand, it's a loving celebration of Angeli. At the film's core, though, is the relationship between the artist and his or her creations, and also a contemplation of the broader notion of identity. Identity is fluid, constantly – however subtly – changing during our lifetime. Yet our former selves never fully disappear. They live on within us, despite our best attempts to vanquish them. And characters that Angeli killed off in print (notably the popular Rê Bordosa) continue, as he discovers, to live on inside him.

DOI: 10.1201/9781032683782-41

Chris Robinson: You made this stop-motion short film *Dossiê Rê Bordosa* (2008) and the series *Angeli "The Killer"* (2017). That would require some passion for the subject! When did you first develop an interest in Angeli? What is it about him and his work that appeals to you?

Cesar Cabral: I grew up reading comics, mainly *Chiclete com Banana* magazine ('*Bubblegum and Banana*'), which means eating bananas and bubblegum at the same time. That was a great influence on my entire generation. It was in this magazine that used to be sold on newsstands that I found a production that spoke directly to my desires and discoveries in counterculture.

The magazine was a mix of comics, literature, music, and pop culture in general. When I started working with animation, my first short *Dossiê Rê Bordosa* was born from the desire to approach Angeli's universe and create a mix of animation and documentary. At that time, I would never have imagined that this would unfold in different works.

Did you always envision a feature film, or did this idea emerge out of the short film or series?

The idea came up in a conversation with Angeli right after making the short. Until then, I considered it impossible to produce such a complex project in terms of costs and execution time. But I believe that the political moment we were living in, with all the investments in ANCINE (the Brazilian cinema agency) and the now-extinct Ministry of Culture, kind of let us dream that it was possible, and after lots of dedication and hard work, we saw the idea materialising.

The intention of producing the feature was born even before the series, which was in fact a direct invitation from Canal Brasil, a private TV company that focuses on independent national productions.

We see fairly consistent animation feature production in Brazil. Based on what I see in the credits, it's a balance between different levels of government support mixed with private funding. Is it easier to fund a feature, which has more distribution potential, than a short film?

Bob Spit, like most Brazilian productions over the last two decades, was financed through public investments from different governmental sectors, since education and the arts and culture sectors were of great importance to the governments that followed since the late 1990s.

The film was financed by the city and state of São Paulo, but mainly by the federal government through tax incentive systems that used important public companies such as the oil corporation Petrobras, the national development bank BNDES, and the FSA (the national film fund). Short films were not allowed to reach this financial system, but we used to get some calls from the Ministry of Culture and local governments, as well as São Paulo's state-owned media development company Spcine.

Over the last three years, to be more precise, all this structure and the entire complex system created in the last decades were dismantled by the current federal government, and now most producers either have co-productions with TV and streaming or have closed their doors.

At the core of *Bob Spit* is the relationship between an artist and his art. In this case, it's a relationship between the artist and his alter ego. Some of what Angeli says reminds me of the writer Hunter S. Thompson, who once acknowledged the myth about him having finally taken over from reality. Is there a danger when the creation becomes, in a sense, the creator?

Angeli's nonconformism is one of his issues, so allowing a pre-established work to take care of his artistic production is something he finds unacceptable. Angeli didn't want to be the guy who made Rê Bordosa or Bob Spit only. His work is constantly changing; he is always aware of the passage of time, and in some ways, in order to move forward, he must disassociate himself from his past.

It doesn't mean that he will disconnect completely, but that this imposed distance will force him to find new paths. As he himself says in the film, the author is the one who must control his creation, and if he cannot, it is better to murder him!

On that line, Angeli the creator is now Angeli the character of Cabral's creation! How challenging is that when your character is a real person?

Yeah! It was a challenge to create a character from a real person and with a pre-established creative universe. What we did was to maintain a dialogue with reality through the material produced in conversations with Angeli, and to work with one of his actual creations, *The Old Cartoonist*, in favour of the narrative, creating a caricature of the author and how he relates to his characters.

And what about the audience? In a sense, all art, once distributed, becomes owned by the audience. Does the artist or their intentions even matter?

I think that making an artistic work comes from the desire of its creator to express something in which he himself has a particular interest, but that also generates public interest in that portrayed universe. So the first thing that calls the attention of the audience is this, but what will be made of it depends on the perspective that each one can have on the subject.

What was the context of the interview with Angeli? Did you record it as a 'normal' interview or was it recorded specifically for the film you envisioned?

At first, I started the interviews in the classic way, with a list of questions and a team that was limited to a camera operator and a recording engineer. Throughout the conversations, which lasted about two years, I adapted and approached Angeli in a more intimate way, looking for conversations that did not have ready answers but that could bring something closer to his personal life and artistic process.

In a way, the fictional part of the film was shaped by the documentary process and vice-versa. I think it is important to point out that there are no dialogues written for Angeli. Everything that appears in the film comes from this documentary process, even though we build *The Old Cartoonist* in his fictional performances.

Did you always know that the interview story would be done in clay animation? Did you ever consider doing it as a live-action film? Or would that have made merging the two stories too difficult and maybe a bit disjointed?

From the beginning, it was clear to me that it should be a claymation. I did the same in *Dossiê Rê Bordosa*. But even considering the stop-motion technique, I wanted to keep things close to reality, in a way that always reminds the audience that we are dealing with the real world. Whether it's a microphone in the scene, a camera that loses focus, or even more realistic acting in the animation, these elements gave credibility to the real, while at the same time, they allowed a connection with the fictional world of its characters.

I knew from the beginning that the film would culminate in an encounter between the creator and his creation, but I always tried to maintain the dilemma of "where fiction begins and reality ends."

How hands-off was Angeli? I would imagine you know him well enough after the short and series, but does he just sit back and trust where you're taking it? He's being interviewed but has no idea what the eventual context of that interview will be. I would imagine it might be hard for Angeli, as an artist, to stop himself from getting involved in the creative process.

Angeli always made a point of making it clear that the film was an artistic process of mine and my team, and therefore he wouldn't involve himself directly, but I believe that this freedom and trust were conquered since the *Dossiê Rê Bordosa* short. The works I created with Angeli always sought a dialogue with the universe he created, but I must admit that showing anything we created to him is always difficult and delicate for me.

Were you surprised by the film's success? Certainly, it would be attractive to Angeli's fans, but *Bob Spit* also captured the attention of many audiences that perhaps didn't know him at all. What do you think was the appeal for those audiences?

As I said before, it is very difficult to imagine how a film will be received, and I was very unsure about the reactions of the international audiences, since I knew they were unaware of Angeli's work or his importance to the political and cultural formation of my generation in my country. But I was also worried if this kind of dark comedy, and the kind of anarchism that Bob Spit represents, would work nowadays.

For the first doubt, Angeli's not being internationally recognized, we decided to invest in a narrative that could reinforce the idea of a middle-aged artist in crisis with his work. For the second, with Bob Spit and the other characters' rebellious and nonsense personalities, we really took the risk.

To tell you the truth, we are proud of the good reception. Maybe it is due to the fact that the film deals with universal themes: it's an author in crisis with his work versus a punk that doesn't accept the imposed reality. In a way, these themes unfold in a broader way in young people's nonconformity with the pre-established reality, or our frustrations with the world we live in or believe in. I think this is synthesized with pop-devouring punk, for example.

Speaking of Angeli's fans, did you get feedback from that community? Were they happy with the film, or did they have unsolicited notes to share with you?

The film was well-received by Angeli's fans. There is a nostalgia that is not limited to the characters, but [linked also] to the music and references that we brought from that time. It is always very delicate to work with characters that have already been consolidated, whether due to the transformation of the 2D line into a 3D sculpture or even the voice we give each character.

The most significant comment I received was that Bob should spit more throughout the film, because, after all, he has a lot to dispute. But I preferred to leave the 'spit' for a special moment in the story, and leave the continuation of the story to the audience!

Remembering Bordo (2022)

42

Borivoj Dovniković-Bordo, one of the most respected and influential filmmakers to emerge from the famous Zagreb school of animation, passed away on February 8, 2022, at the age of 91.

Bordo, as he was known to most, was born on December 12, 1930, in Osijek, Croatia (then Yugoslavia). Aged around 19, he moved to Zagreb to study at the Academy of Fine Arts. A year later, he joined the satirical weekly *Kerempuh* as one of the caricaturists. The magazine was popular, and the editor, Fadil Hadžić, was inspired to put some of those profits into a satirical animation short.

The result was *The Big Meeting* (1951), directed by Norbert Neugebauer, and animated and designed by his brother Walter. Among the many animation assistants was Bordo. That same year, Hadžić founded Duga Film. Bordo, along with future Zagreb Film animators Zlatko Grgić, Vlado Kristl, and Dušan Vukotić, joined the effort. He worked on five films before the studio folded in 1952, after the Croatian government diverted funding to education and healthcare.

A few years after the demise of Duga, Zagreb Film emerged. Influenced by UPA and the National Film Board of Canada among others, the animation studio would become among the most influential around the globe. Zagreb Film was noted for its unique graphic styles, limited animation, and exploration of themes like war, society, and the problem of being a human in an often chaotic, nonsensical world.

Bordo made his directorial debut in 1961 with *The Doll*, but it was *Without Title* (1964) that started to bring attention to his work. This satire of bureaucracy, about a man whose efforts to be in a film are continually blocked by the opening and ending credits, won an award at Oberhausen.

From the start, Bordo's work is preoccupied with regular guys making their way in a rather surreal and frequently interfering world. Each film starts with a gag and then riffs on it. Bordo's films are also noted for their satirical punch, and minimal use of dialogue and design, occasionally mixed with collage.

DOI: 10.1201/9781032683782-42

Ceremony (1965) is a dark satire in which a group of guys pose for a picture during a ceremony that turns out to be a firing-squad execution. *In Curiosity* (1966), a man sits on a park bench with a mysterious paper bag. A parade of people (workers, school kids, cyclists, cruise-ship occupants) become curious to the point of intrusiveness, desperate to find out what it is in this bag.

In *Krek* (1968), winner of the Silver Bear at the Berlin Film Festival, we follow a man who joins the army and brings his pet frog along. To the annoyance of his commanding officer, the frog continually distracts the man from his duties by taking him into a world of consumerist fantasy. *The Flower Lovers* (1970) is about a community that becomes fixated on exploding flowers. In *Second Class Passenger* (1974), a man encounters all sorts of oddballs (dogs, aliens, cowboys, astronauts, soccer players) during a train ride.

One Day of Life (1982) is a simple, compassionate portrait of a factory worker who briefly interrupts his dreary, repetitive existence by getting hammered at a local pub with an old friend. *Exciting Love Story* (1989) veers a bit away, formally at least, from his previous films. The screen is divided into eight frames and a man travels within each frame in search of his love, Gloria.

Midhat 'Ajan' Ajanović, an animation scholar, teacher, and author, says that Bordo's stories

> always revolved around a goodhearted, affectionate, and naïve 'little man' who would find himself in trouble because of something totally unnatural and illogical, or due to human wickedness. Drawn figures proved to be perfect 'actors,' which transferred with great precision the author's vision of an ordinary little man and his 'struggle to live an ordinary life.'

Echoing the stubborn, determined traits of Buster Keaton or Charlie Chaplin, Bordo's characters are not pushovers. "After having undergone molestation in the first part of the film," says Ajanović, "the character experiences a catharsis and transforms into a real fighter who refuses to be terrorized any longer. His ordinary men become totally extraordinary."

Ajanović continues:

> As far as figure design and drawing technique were concerned, Bordo, like Grgić and fellow Zagreb artist Nedeljko Dragić, was strongly influenced by Saul Steinberg's purity and simplicity. Bordo was somewhat older than his colleagues, so his drawing style retained plasticity, volume, and a softness of line, placing his graphics halfway between Disney and Steinberg. As an animator, he was relaxed. His drawings were copied from the paper onto the cel with an unequally thick line that constantly pulsated on the screen, creating a lively and irresistible film image.

Beyond his films, Bordo played an instrumental role in the founding of Animafest Zagreb in 1972, now one of the world's best-known animated festivals,. He not only co-created the festival's logo and first signal film but was also president of the programming committee in the early 1980s. From 1985–1991, he served as the festival director.

Margit 'Buba' Antauer, who was the festival's managing director from 1992–2006, recalls,

> I met Bordo almost 50 years ago, during my first Animafest engagement. He was one of the founders and leading people of that special event that penetrated my blood and is still filling my heart with special energy. Bordo immediately had my respect and admiration.

Many people were influenced by his animation book *Škola crtanog filma* ('School of Animated Film'), including animator and current Animafest artistic director Daniel Šuljić. "When I started as an animation student in Vienna, I did a lot of exercises based on his instructions from that book, and I know that other people did the same," Šuljić said in a statement.

> He taught us how to walk, just as the name of one of his best films, *Learning to Walk,* says. Bordo left us his films, simple, based on gags (as Ronald Holloway stated in his book *Z is for Zagreb*), but always deeply human, in the love of a 'small' man.

Andrijana Ružić, an animation historian and author, concurs:

> From that book, I have finally understood the meaning of a secret ingredient in an animated film—the famous timing. Bordo himself was a master of timing, and it is evident in his witty and sour shorts that he treated the everyday troubles of an ordinary man. His films are never consolatory, but what can console us really, in the end? Very few animators knew how to create the right timing of an ordinary man's life like Bordo did.

Antauer fondly recalls sharing some time with Bordo at the Animator's Picnic at Animafest's 2021 edition:

> By chance, I could hear the words he was imparting to young student animators who gathered around him, knowing that they were lucky to meet a true animation legend. He told them, "Almost my whole life I not only dreamed, but I deeply believed that if we really try hard, animation will help us to reach the stars!" And you did it, dear friend. You did it, and now you are one of them! And you will shine forever! Bordo, our superstar!

Editing *Flee* (2022)

43

Flee, an animated feature film by Jonas Poher Rasmussen, is about a man, Amin, recounting his experience of being forced to flee Afghanistan while also struggling with his sexuality. The film is a fascinating and poignant work that fuses documentary, animation, and archival footage over very distinct segments that shift between Amir's present as he recounts his story to a friend and the recreation of Amir's past experiences.

The fact that *Flee* is nominated for best documentary feature, animation feature, and international film speaks volumes about the creators' success in blending different visual styles, tones, and paces.

To glean insight into the challenges of working with documentary and animation elements, I spoke with *Flee*'s award-winning editor, Janus Billeskov Jansen (*Another Round, Pusher II, The Hunt, The Best Intentions*) via Zoom. Jansen, who has been Denmark's go-to film editor for decades, discussed how he collaborated with the director to construct the narrative, the film's impactful ending shot, and the hard work of integrating archival footage, audio recording, and animation into a fully-realised whole.

Chris Robinson: You have decades of editing experience working on documentaries and live-action films, so how did *Flee* end up in your lap?

Janus Billeskov Jansen: I knew Jonas [Poher Rasmussen] from his time at film school. He was at a different kind of film school in Denmark called Super 16. It was created 20 years ago or so by a group of young people who had been refused by the Danish Film School. So they created their own school, and it has actually grown into a very interesting and successful alternative film school in Denmark. So I knew Jonas from there because I would sometimes teach there. I was also involved in his last project at the school. Later, he continued working on documentaries, and I would occasionally help supervise the editing process of his work and give him my reactions.

DOI: 10.1201/9781032683782-43

Flee ended up at Final Cut For Real, a production company I am a part owner of with Signe Byrge Sørensen. So it was very natural that we started to work together. He came to us with these ideas about seven years ago. It started out as an ordinary documentary. Later, it turned into an animation. And it was very interesting, because it would have been very difficult to do a regular documentary. Not just because Amin wanted to be anonymous, but because it would have been very complicated to film and to get footage from different periods of time.

Can you talk about your role as editor of *Flee*? In CG animation, for example, the editor is involved in planning, whereas in a more traditional film, the editor generally does a lot of the work after the footage is done.

Jansen: Yes, I was there from the beginning. When they first started talking about it as an animation, they laid out the characters. We were doing a lot of editing for a film that has not yet been shot. We had all these dialogues between Jonas and Amin that we put together in lines of voices and then animated on top of those a little later. We went back and forth a lot. We changed the rhythm of the story, the order of the scenes, and we also condensed it more. This was important for production because the film animatic we delivered had to be the exact length. For me, it was really to use all my skills from 50 years of editing and to say, "How long are we going to be on this shot?" "Should it be a wide shot?" "Should it be closer?"

When they started talking about it being an animated film, they laid out the individual characters, just to show what they could look like at different ages. We had some of the layout of some of the re-enactment parts, and we had a huge amount of archived material from different places. Jonas had already gone out and done a lot of research. And he went out to find the original buildings to see if there was any archival material around. But that developed during the editing. We had started editing the scene where the two sisters go with human traffickers and end up in Stockholm on this ship.

What we didn't have was the part where the man was on the sinking ship before being taken into custody and placed in this terrible prison. It was during the editing that we found the actual footage. Amin remembered seeing a television crew there and thought they might have come from Finland. So we actually found the original footage and Amin recognized all the different people. So that particular scene grew and became a bigger story. Jonas had to go back and interview Amin to focus on more details from that particular moment.

The whole setup of Amin lying on the couch there with the camera, where you see the camera and you have this top camera on his face, that is one-to-one. It was something that you could actually animate on top of. What we do with this kind of dialogue is to shorten it, compress it, and make it more clear for the actual story. Which we normally do for every kind of documentary. There's nothing strange about that. But when we animated, we could do it as one scene without any cuts in it. Although throughout the film, we have these out-of-continuity cuts where it's jumping in the animation. We didn't necessarily have to do that; we could have smoothened it all out, but we wanted to keep the audience aware that this is actually a documentary film, a true story.

So, Amin must have been heavily involved in the re-enactment parts, since it's his memories being re-enacted and animated.

Jansen: It's something that went back and forth between Amin and Jonas as the director. I decided that I would not really meet Amin. I wanted to be in the same position as the audience. But throughout the editing, we realized that we had a lot of different pieces that we needed to explore more. Things like the inner life of the boy. So, then Jonas would go back and forth with the particular purpose of digging more into that part of Amin's past. Those were not filled with cameras, but it was a similar setup. Amin was lying down, with two microphones set up. The way that you talk is different when standing, sitting, or lying down.

There was also the issue of getting into Amin's memory. He didn't necessarily know what Jonas wanted. The important thing in this storytelling is that you want to have that feeling in his voice that he is digging into his memory. And the way the voice floats there is an important part of what this film is about. This is Amin's real voice, and on top of that is animation. So it's like these two elements are talking together, and out of that comes something completely new. And that's very interesting. When we deal with his conversation with Jonas or his voice-over in explaining some of the different animated scenes, the tone is so important. And this was something Jonas and I carefully orchestrated throughout the editing.

How much live-action footage did you have? What kinds of discussions were there about balancing the live action with the animation?

Jansen: All of the backstory, the childhood, was all totally animated. There's no original footage for that. In the conversation on the couch, there was a lot of footage, but there was also a lot of recorded talk that wasn't filmed. In the interaction between Amin and his boyfriend, a lot of it was filmed. That kind of dialogue was actually happening for real, and then they animated on top of that. But we also had to get deeper into the emotional situation at times and had to add new lines there.

What I've always said about documentaries is that we use 90% of the editing time to figure out what the exact ending of the film is. So many times, the beginning and end of the film are the most complicated things. With *Flee*, this wasn't a problem. Jonas had sorted it out from the very beginning.

Let's talk about the ending. The final shot is quite powerful, but it could have potentially come across as a bit sentimental or forced. Instead, it's like a bridge between animation and reality. It's really, again, reminding the audience that this isn't some fictional cartoon, this is a true story about a real person.

Jansen: We discussed the last shot a couple of times. A couple of minutes before that, they had decided to move in together. Moving into a house is taking responsibility for each other. That's the implication of it. So, we had that scene and that was actually shot so that the dialogue there was really happening in that emotional situation. But the interesting thing there is that the film is operating on two levels: He is the grown-up lying on the couch talking about his childhood and family story and struggling with these secrets he's been keeping about his homosexuality. That's one thing.

But it's also a story about a grown-up man lying on a couch telling his childhood story, and by doing that, it's doing something to him in the present. What kind of knowledge and reflection does it give him for his life going forward? And that was something we needed to go further into throughout the editing of the film. So that really suddenly expanded and it was very interesting to work with that part of it. Secrets aside, you also have this burden that's been placed on Amin's shoulder. He was the one who got opportunities, and he felt pressured to succeed for his family.

Well, that final shot nicely reflects that, because you get this subtle transition from animation to live action. It's almost like it's time for Amin to let go and start living his own life.

Jansen: There's a parallel to the earlier scene where they are looking for a house, but Amin clearly doesn't want any part of it. So the last scene mirrors that one because now they're connected finally. We almost cut that earlier scene. We thought it might be a little boring, but at an early screening, people reacted very strongly and really understood it. Also, for the final shot, we did have live footage before.

Yes, it was archival footage that was squared in on the canvas with some historical distance, but I think it prepared the audience for the final shot.

What did you come away with after working with animation? Was there something that may have surprised or challenged you?

Jansen: For me, in feature films, we normally start editing throughout the shooting. So you can go back and ask for additional shots or things like that. They are in a hurry and it costs money, so when you ask for something, you really have to think carefully and not ask too much. But with *Flee*, it's just saying, "Oh, shouldn't we have a wide shot of Kabul before we actually get into the scene with the mother and sisters around the table there?" Then they just say, "Okay." If that was a live shot, it would be complicated and expensive, but here they can just draw it.

What I think was a tough thing was to be sure that the length of the shots in this very rough first animation was what they should be in the final film. That was a unique experience.

And then another thing that was interesting was that it was close to the end of the editing. We had a couple of screenings with these rough black-and-white images on the screen. What was fantastic was that it still moved the audience, some to tears. At first, I got a little scared because I thought, if these black and white, very poorly animated pieces can take the audience by the heart, will the fully animated version still have the same effect? Can it live up to the audience's imagination? But it turned out to be very good. The animation really gave Amin a fantastic character.

It's Not Just the Beginning

44

Animation Has Always Pushed Boundaries (2022)

Where to begin with that narcissist foul-up called the Oscars?

First, we had the Academy's decision not to televise a bunch of categories, including the award for best animated short. Then, during the Oscars, three Disney actresses came on to announce the animated feature winner. First, they did their Disney duty by plugging their past and future Disney film roles (all this happening on a Disney-owned network). Then, these three *animation historians* went on to tell the world how animation is first and foremost a kid's thing. All this before eventually announcing the winner, which, what a surprise, turned out to be a Disney film.

But, those issues have already been discussed here.

One moment that might have slipped past people was the comments made by Alberto Mielgo after winning the short animation Oscar for *The Windshield Wiper*.

Now it didn't start too bad. You can't quarrel with Mielgo's opening remarks that rightly claimed animation includes every art form and that "adult animation is a fact." It was his closing line that rankled me: "This is just the beginning of what we can do with animation."

I really got the impression that he thinks he's somehow radically reinventing animation and that adult-oriented animation did not exist before. I have nothing against Mielgo. I don't think he was doing anything malicious, but it

DOI: 10.1201/9781032683782-44

was a naïve and incorrect comment. (In a separate interview I did with Oscar nominees for a different publication, he talked about how being nominated showed that the Academy was finally taking adult animation seriously, which is just not true.)

Let's be clear: This is *not* the beginning of what can be done with animation. That's been happening for decades, maybe centuries. It's always happening.

How do I know?

Well, a little background.

I've been involved in animation for 30 years as a writer, author, and as the artistic director of the Ottawa International Animation Festival (OIAF). My job (unbelievably) is essentially to watch over 2,000 animation films (of all shapes and sizes) annually and select the best ones for festival programs. In short, I see a lot of animation.

During this time, I've made it a priority to find innovative voices. I was always bothered by the way animation festivals (including the OIAF) tended to prioritize films for how they looked rather than what they had to say. Too often, I saw films that were beautifully crafted but had (in my view) absolutely nothing interesting or unique to say. I tried (and still try) to shift away from craft and technique and prioritize what a film is saying. A great example might be JJ Villard's now classic student film, *Son of Satan*. It's an ugly film with distorted audio, but behind that was a potent punk riff about bullying and domestic abuse. There was an urgency to that film that is too often missing in animation. In short, I've done my best to seek out and share unsung and overlooked voices—and there were and are plenty.

So when I hear someone talk as though animation was somehow never mature, relevant, or provocative until now, well, yeah, I take issue.

First off, all you need to do is glance over at some of Mielgo's fellow nominees: *Bestia* (about a torturer), *Affairs of the Art* (about a dysfunctional family), *Boxballet* (about a love affair between a boxer and a ballerina that maybe touches upon some issues of gender stereotypes). Aside from *Robin, Robin*, all the nominees were aimed at adult audiences. And as problematic as Oscar selections are (they do not accurately reflect the state and quality of the animation world), adult or art-house animation has always had some place (however small) at the Oscars.

If that doesn't convince you, well, maybe go to some animation festivals where one can regularly see experimental, poetic, and personal works that deal with an array of non-kiddie subjects: domestic abuse (*Steakhouse*), mental illness (*A Family That Steals Dogs*), adultery/murder (*Night Bus*), rape (*Granny's Sex Life*), colonization, abuse, assimilation (*Meneath*), transgender issues (*All Those Sensations in My Belly*).

That's just a minuscule sampling from the last year. I haven't even started travelling back through animation history to toss out endless examples of radical animation: McLaren, Lye, Fischinger, Vanderbeek, Griffin, Bakshi, Baumane, Norstein, Pärn, Koyalyov, Mulloy, Hykade, Cournoyer, Tilby/ Forbis, Landreth, Hobbs… I mean, I could go on and on with examples.

And look, *The Windshield Wiper* is a commendable work, worthy of attention, but the idea that it's something bold and groundbreaking is more than a bit of a stretch. *The Windshield Wiper* isn't some radical, pioneering work that is changing the animation landscape. Mielgo might want to spend a bit more time checking out animation and short-film festivals, where you'd find so much fresh and intriguing work that you'd see that 'adult' animation is the norm, not the exception.

In that context, I find Mielgo's comment (however innocent) as problematic as the other issues of the evening. It denied animation history. It rejected what exists, has existed, and will continue to exist. The remark also inadvertently reaffirmed the exhausting and erroneous belief that animation is, at its core, nothing more than entertainment.

At what point do animators wake up and realize they're in an abusive relationship? Year after year, animators crave love from the Academy only to be let down and treated as afterthoughts. If this year didn't drive that sad truth home, well, there's not much to be done, I'm afraid.

Clearly, though, Chris Rock wasn't the only one who got slapped in the face.

Lei Lei

Navigating The Personal Side of Chinese History (2022)

45

Lei Lei, a Chinese animator, artist, and musician, has been making films for just over 10 years now. Using a mixed-media approach that combined cutouts, collage elements, and drawings, Lei Lei's vibrant candy-coloured tales of love and diversity brought instant acclaim. Since then, the filmmaker has established himself as one of the most refreshing and unique voices on the animation circuit.

Beginning with the film *Recycled* and its follow-up *Hand Coloured #2*, both co-directed with Thomas Sauvin, Lei Lei's work took on a new direction. While his earlier films always utilized collage elements, his later work has expanded on that by incorporating hundreds of found photographs collected from assorted Chinese flea markets. In both films, Lei Lei turns his eye from fantasy stories towards a sort of resuscitation of personal Chinese stories often suppressed, censored, or erased by turbulent Chinese policies.

In his most recent feature, the US/Dutch co-production *Silver Bird and Rainbow Fish*, Lei Lei continues this exploration of Chinese history, this time visiting his own family roots. Using interviews with his father and grandfather (who died before the film was finished), *Silver Bird and Rainbow Fish* follows the story of four-year-old Jiaqi (Lei Lei's father). After the boy's mother dies, his father (Lei Lei's grandfather) is forced to put him and his sister in an orphanage while he seeks work in the countryside. Eventually, they are all reunited by a new woman who emerges in their lives.

DOI: 10.1201/9781032683782-45

Silver Bird and Rainbow Fish is Lei Lei's most visually and conceptually ambitious work yet and made on a modest budget of around US$900,000. Straddling the borders of animation and documentary while blurring the lines between personal memory, history, and fiction (many of the photos are not of Lei Lei's family), he mixes archival photography, collage elements, hand painting, and clay as he transports us back to a rather chaotic 1960s China.

Through this approach, Lei Lei acts as a sort of animation Dr. Frankenstein, patching together forgotten and erased voices, faces, and experiences to tell a story that is at once deeply personal and relatable to many who experienced a similar sometimes-tumultuous existence in China. What's equally interesting is that while the film is dominated by male voices, it's the women (specifically Lei Lei's step-grandmother) who prove to be the real pillars of strength.

"Actually, the two animals signify two female characters in the film," Lei Lei recounted during a Zoom interview.

> When translated into English, the original Chinese title means second and third mother. It was very hard to find a name in English. *Silver Bird and the Rainbow Fish* jumped into my mind one day. I think it's very lovely and romantic.

The roots of the film's aesthetic, strangely, can be found in Quebec City, Canada. "I was doing a residency there and intended to make a short film based on interviews with my grandfather."

Lei Lei had brought along a colourful collection of clay to tinker with during those long, dark, lonely Canadian winters.

> Clay, for me, is totally new. Before I went to Quebec City, I had no idea what kind of material I would use in this film. I knew it was about my family's history, but I didn't have any photos or home movies that I could access. Then, I thought I could just make it all with my hands, create mountains, rivers and people with clay.

Not surprisingly, given the lack of material, most of the archival photos used in the film are not of Lei Lei's family. He elaborated, "Except for the photo album at the beginning and end of the film, the photos are all of strangers. They are photos I collected from second-hand fairs."

It's this blurring between private and public, family and nation, that elevates *Silver Bird and Rainbow Fish* from being a strictly personal family diary. It becomes not just a story of one family, but of many Chinese families, or anyone who experienced restrictive governments.

The film is not, however, a heavy-handed exploration of personal and collective social and cultural histories. Lei Lei's comic tendencies frequently appear in *Silver Bird*. In one playful scene in which Lei Lei must pause the interview with his father, instead of just cutting out the intervening silence Lei Lei lets the tape run while the viewer and his father await Lei Lei's return.

> I think that because I had a lot of time to communicate with my family and know our background, there was freedom. I'm not standing on the stage telling everyone my story. This was a shared experience between my family and the audience.

Later, his grandfather provides Lei Lei with concise feedback about an early, shorter cut of the film: "It's good, but not good enough."

It's these playful moments and the obvious love between the family members that give the film a uniquely playful, intimate, and almost interactive vibe. Throughout the film, the audience feels part of a lively conversation, a seatmate at a table in some pub listening to raconteurs casually regaling the audience with fragmented tales from the past.

And of course, these conversations between grandfather, father, and son were and are very meaningful for Lei Lei. Maybe around 2017 or 2018, my grandfather saw part of the film, but he was in bad health. Later, when I finished the film, I went back to my hometown and watched it together with my father. He loved it. He said he had never watched animation in this way before.

In keeping with the spirit of collage, Lei Lei was also able to create a special moment for his father.

> I cut out my father's voice and placed it with my grandfather's voice, so it gives the impression that they are having a new conversation together. My father was very emotional about this part. He said it was very beautiful to bring my grandfather back.

After working on the film on-and-off for six years, Lei Lei is happy with what he achieved.

> *Silver Bird and Rainbow Fish* is very important to me because if you say *Recycled* is very different from *This Is Love* (2010), then I think *Silver Bird* tries to bring in a different technique. I continue to think about my cinematic language and how to use cutout and collage together with archive documentary materials. So, yeah, I'm happy I finished this project. It's like a finished promise I made to myself.

It Never Felt So Good (2022)

46

From reindeer and hedgehogs to robins, anxiety monsters, and poor ol' Willy, the use of felt in animation has taken on a whole new energy in recent years. While some point to Emma de Swaef and Marc Roels' *Oh Willy...* (2012) as a sort of pioneer, the use of felt material in animation was popular long before either of the Belgian duo was conceived.

Many animators have dabbled with felt in the past, including Czech animators Hermína Týrlová and Bratislav Pojar (*Hey Mister, Let's Play*). Earlier still, Ladislav Starewich used it to animate a cat in *The Tale of the Fox*. The cult-classic Christmas special *Rudolph the Red-Nosed Reindeer* (Rankin/Bass) used felt puppets that combined wood, felted wool, and wire. Later, the 1980s series *The Moomins* used felt as well.

That said, *Oh Willy...* seems to have kickstarted a renewed interest in the material. It certainly demonstrated a different texture of felt from previous examples. There's a loose, rougher quality to the characters that can also be seen in films like *The Magnificent Cake*, *But Milk is Important*, and other works.

So, attempting to discover what's so appealing about working with felt and why so many are doing so now, I asked a handful of specialist animators for their opinions, good or bad, about the material.

EMMA DE SWAEF (*OH WILLY..., THE MAGNIFICENT CAKE, THE HOUSE*)

We use a very cheap mix of wool and acrylic that I can only find in a specific shop in Manchester, in sheets. We press the sheets of wool into a shape like a hatmaker would, as opposed to needle-felting it. I discovered it while visiting Mackinnon and Saunders while developing *Oh Willy...* back in 2010. I've tried a few different types of felt from different sources but I like the exact shade of pink and thickness of this one, though I would prefer it if it was more flexible. So, I stuck with it over the years, even making city trips to Manchester just to go to the otherwise unremarkable store that sells it. After every film, we do feel like

DOI: 10.1201/9781032683782-46

we're really hitting the limit though and are considering using different types or textiles. I'm particularly frustrated at how it limits mouth and eyebrow movement, and how it starts fraying around the edges of mouths when pushed too far.

We mainly like how it interacts with light. It allows for a stylization of the human form, away from the uncanny valley. Because of the texture, it's always obvious that the technique is stop motion, never looks like 3D. We try to work with the limitations it gives us on the character animation level in writing and 'decoupage.' I'm also just very comfortable with the material generally. I've worked with wool from a very young age, we had sheep when I was young. I probably have my '10,000 hours' with it now, a skill and familiarity that feels like a pity to let go of or deviate from.

ANNA MANTZARIS (*BUT MILK IS IMPORTANT* – CO-DIRECTED WITH EIRIK GRØNMO BJØRNSEN, *ENOUGH, GOOD INTENTIONS*)

At the moment I'm using felt sheets made from both real and synthetic wool. I do the heads in balsa wood or Super Sculpy clay and then cover them in the felt sheets. It has changed. For *Milk*, we used a needle felting technique which we first tried in a needle felting workshop in Tallinn. Also, my mom has always done needle-felted characters for the kindergarten where she works. Needle felting gives a fluffier look which suited the creature in that film. Later, I became inspired by others who used it on human characters as well, such as the creators of *Oh Willy....* But for that, I used felt sheets as it's a bit more compact and better for making details. I like it because it gives a soft touch to the characters, and it allows me to keep a simple style without the characters feeling stiff or harsh. It sort of humanizes them and softens them up, I think. It's also quite an easy and quick technique, compared to casting things in silicone and resin etc. The only downside is that it's hard to clean when it gets dirty.

EVA CVIJANOVIĆ (*HEDGEHOG'S HOME*)

I used felted wool. Nothing super special. We used some local wool from a Croatian farmer and some nice Merino wool for the colours. Wool is warm and fuzzy; it brings those warm fuzzy feelings we want for a film about home. The quote that always came up was that I wanted it to 'feel like a warm blanket.'

That and the fact that it has beautiful bright colours and a folky feel which went well with the story and with the style of the original illustrations. Also technically, wool is lightweight so a great material for animation. Doesn't weigh the armature down like plasticine for example.

ANDREA LOVE (*TULIP*, CO-DIRECTED WITH PHOEBE WAHL, *COOKING WITH WOOL* SERIES)

I mostly use wool roving for 3-dimensional needle felting, but I incorporate fabric felt in various ways as well. I have a deep obsession with wool roving as it applies to stop motion. It's lightweight, malleable, has a directional grain, and interesting variations in colour and texture. It's surprisingly good at holding a shape and can execute particle effects like fire, water, and smoke. It can achieve a high level of realism, but it also shines in abstract and surreal settings. I like that it gives people a tactile, visceral reaction. Most people find it comforting and nostalgic, but there's another group of people who feel itchy and uncomfortable and can't stand it. Many people don't even know what they are looking at when they watch needle-felted animation, so it takes on a bit of a magical feel. I'm surprised needle felting isn't a more popular mainstream craft, but perhaps it is going in that direction as people learn more about it!

ROBIN JENSEN (NORWEGIAN ASSOCIATION OF THE BLIND AND PARTIALLY SIGHTED, *HELP! WE HAVE A BLIND PATIENT*)

The material I used was old stockings. The whole idea of using puppets instead of, let's say classic cartoon, cutout, or even 3D, was because I thought it would emphasize the problems of being blind. It just felt more 'real' if the puppets actually existed. The consequences of their action would feel more painful in a way instead of, let's say, if a drawn character fell down the stairs. I don´t know if that's true, but that was the idea. The reason for using old stockings was for several reasons, money being one of them. We needed to make the puppets fast and cheap, so this just seemed to be the easiest thing to do. The puppets didn't even have a professional armature. They are just made with strings, causing a bit of a pain for the animator (Margrethe Danielsen). But she was also the one who made the puppets, so it all worked out fine.

ŠPELA ČADEŽ (*ORANGE IS THE NEW BLACK – UNRAVELED*)

I used felt because it was easy, fast and cheap. We needed 23 puppets in three weeks. And somehow felt is warm in contrast to the brutal prison those girls were in. I first thought I'm going to needle felt them, but then I realized it was way better to make them out of fabric felt, it just needed to be real wool. I was lucky to be in Holland at the festival and there was a store with really great wool felt. So I bought all the felt there. In Ljubljana, they had only one that was mixed with plastic. Felt fabric can be well formed with steam and the camera loves it. The light has to be soft, and it all looks great.

DALE HAYWARD (CO-DIRECTOR WITH SYLVIE TROUVÉ) AND DAPHNÉ LOUBOT (PUPPET FABRICATION WITH DOMINIQUE COTÉ) (*A PLACE FOR ALL OF US, LES ÉMERVEILLEURS*)

Loubot: We mostly felted with water but also needle felted. It was Merino wool for the video clip and mostly carded wool for the advertisement. Merino is a type of wool from Merino sheep and carded is a way to treat the wool. Carded also means felted, in that case, it's kind of 'pre-felted.' So, we use Merino and Bergschaf wool that was carded. Carded wool was faster than felt because a part of the job is already done. Also, the Bergschaf fibers are rougher and easy to felt. For *A Place for All of Us* we wanted a tighter-looking wool, less hairy.

Hayward: The project's main reference was *Hedgehog's Home* (thanks Eva!), so felt felt right from the beginning. The wool texture feels like home; warm and friendly. It's also versatile, it works well as skin, clothes, and objects. Coinciding with the spot, we were also creating a music video for Ingrid St. Pierre, and she also referenced wool characters. So it was very practical from the production standpoint to keep the same crew working. It's also relatively fast to create a good-looking puppet with felt, so that was important too.

MIKEY PLEASE AND DAN OJARI (CO-DIRECTORS), ANNE KING (PUPPET MAKING CREATIVE LEAD) (*ROBIN ROBIN*)

King:

We started by using extra fine Merino, which does felt well, but puppet maker Mariela Sartori, whom we hired as a felt expert, had used a different one which she found superior, so we used that. We used Maori from Dying House Gallery (DHG) in Italy. According to the company, Maori is a blend of carded wool from New Zealand. When we started creating this item back in 2007, we wanted a wool that was perfect for needle felting with a nice natural colour that would allow us to create bright colours as well as soft pastel nuances. After numerous tests, we came up with this blend that is now one of our iconic products, loved by both beginners and the more experienced. We couldn't have chosen a more iconic name: Maori. A small tribute to a great nation and to the homeland of these wools! This was imported in big boxes, and we blended the colours we needed ourselves from their range.

Please and Ojari:

There's something in the way that felt absorbs light that was deeply attractive to us. That slight translucence is a quality we've loved in our previous films, where the material interacts with the environment and feels that little bit more alive. Previously that transparent material had been Plastazote, and we hadn't done a huge deal with felt. But on our second pitch to Aardman, we brought a handful of Christmas decorations with us to demonstrate the material's inherent charm and everyone was on board right away. There are lots of parallels with clay, the traditional material of choice at Aardman, in that it's possible to sculpt and manipulate in a way not possible with silicone or Plastazote. Keeping the puppets malleable allows for heaps of on-the-floor possibilities where you might want a character to hit an extreme pose. We exploited that freedom a lot with characters like the Cat and some of the huge mouth shapes she had to hit.

Saving Israeli Animation (2022)

47

Heading home from this year's Annecy Festival, animators and Israeli Animation Guild representatives Ben Molina and Ayala Sharot were on a high.

They'd spent a week making contacts, seeing films, and promoting the Israeli animation community. When they returned home, even better news was waiting for them: after years of discussion, the Israeli government was finally going to announce a pilot tax credit system for the film industry.

"The government came up with this new plan of subsidizing foreign productions that come to film in Israel," says Sharot. "The idea was to give 30% cash back on all foreign investment coming in."

This initiative, spearheaded by the Ministries of Culture and Sport, Foreign Affairs, Tourism, Economy and Industry, and Finance, was not unlike tax credit systems in many other countries. It was a way to encourage foreign productions and tourism in a country where security concerns and bureaucracy have frequently hindered the film industry.

When the program was finally ready to be officially announced in late June 2022, Molina and Sharot were stunned by the details of the plan: animation had been excluded.

Animation getting the short shift is nothing new. One would be hard-pressed to find a corner of the world where animation is treated on par with its live-action peers. Still, Molina, manager of the Israeli Animation Guild, and Sharot, the Guild chairwoman, were shocked and angered by the government's erasure of animation from its plans.

"In like two words, they erased our entire industry and essence," said Molina. "We were pissed. The Guild jumped right into battle. We sent an email to all the Guild members saying this was a red alert and an animation emergency."

Molina and his associates made phone calls and sent emails to the relevant ministries. They called on union and guild members to send letters to the five ministries responsible for the program. After that,

DOI: 10.1201/9781032683782-47

we approached studio owners, independent animators, teachers, and even the big shots like Ari Folman [*Waltz with Bashir*], Etgar Keret [*A Brief History of Us*], and Gidi Dar [*Legend of Destruction*]. We also managed to get the director, screenwriters, and producer guilds to sign a petition.

"As soon as people realized what we were doing, they just volunteered to help," added Sharot.

One of our community members – a brilliant director and a mother of two children – spent a whole weekend at her computer collecting data, making phone calls to studio owners, and then creating this fantastic document for us. Everyone did their own little part, and it really brought the community together.

Once they had their petitions and data, they approached the various ministries. First up was the Ministry of Culture and Sport, who quickly realized that they'd made a mistake and threw their full support behind having animation included in the legislation.

In relatively rapid succession the Guild managed – with the help of the Ministry of Culture and Sport – to get Tourism, Economy, and Foreign Affairs on board. That left Finance. But, they were not as easily convinced of animation's economic relevance.

"There were a lot of internal debates," recalled Molina. "It's crazy. I believe it's the first time that the ministries talked with each other about animation. I think that's an incredible achievement on its own."

"Governments talked about cinema but never about animation," Sharot agreed. "That's the same everywhere. We were like, 'Hey guys, there's an industry here and it's art and it's economics and it's good publicity for Israel.'"

Sharot believes the government's definition of cinema is out of date.

The tax credit initiative was started as a way to promote tourism to Israel. If foreign productions came to Israel, [audiences] would see the beautiful landscapes of Israel and maybe come to visit. Of course, you can't really achieve that in animation. So our case was that film production is different today from, say, the 1980s. You film on greenscreens and use visual effects.

Furthering the economic argument, Molina pointed out that,

We saw that a production could employ 30 full-time animators for an entire year. With cinema, it's maybe a few months of shooting and editing, and then you're done and people go back to the market. So, animation has more potential for creating a stable industry.

While appealing to the various ministries, Molina and Sharot were constantly frustrated by the unwillingness of organizations to provide any type of explanation for animation's omission.

"When they ruled out animation, they had no explanation," said Molina. "It seemed like there was something else going on behind the scenes. Someone seems to have asked specifically that animation not be included, and we just don't understand why."

In many countries, there are often internal battles between the live-action, documentary, and animation industries. There's a relatively small pie available to the cinematic arts, and rather than share it equitably, there's usually some group that wants a larger piece.

In late July, just as the Guild was preparing to file a lawsuit, they got a call from the Ministry of Culture telling them to be patient, and that good news was on the way.

The Ministry of Finance had had a change of heart. At the end of July, it was announced that animation would now be included in the new tax credit system. Exhausted, stressed, and emotionally spent, Molina and Sharot were, more than anything, ecstatic.

The entire process proved a revelation.

"The most beautiful thing was that it brought the animation community together," said Sharot. "People are starting to understand that it's an ecosystem that feeds off each other. It's not just one studio that can make it. You need everyone. That's the only way to make the industry grow."

The experience was also a hasty initiation for Molina and Sharot into the messy world of politics. "We started to understand that we have to be politicians," said Molina. "We have to have representation."

Or as Sharot puts it, "Sometimes an artist has to learn to be a politician."

Making Bread with Alex Boya (2022)

48

In the world of entertainment, it often goes that someone creates a work (e.g., *Star Wars*, *The Simpsons*) and it develops a huge following to the point where the audience is so invested in the characters and their worlds that they start imagining their own scenarios for those elements, like with fan fiction. Other times, a narrative work (e.g., *The Boys*, or just about any old comic book) starts out in one form and is adapted and expanded into another.

Canadian animator and artist Alex Boya (*Turbine*) is taking, perhaps, the opposite route. Boya, with the help of Giphy and assorted contributors, has been constructing an expanded universe called *The Mill* to generate interest in an eventual short film and/or series. Not an easy task, but certainly a unique one, and a successful one; Boya's Giphy channel has 2.9 billion views.

"It's basically an experimental world-building project that is expressed in a multi-timeline story," Boya said during a July interview at a Portuguese restaurant in Montreal. "There are different stories simultaneously without linear, cohesive chronology. The main way that this world-building project manifests in reality is through my animation channel posted by Giphy."

The Mill, whose roots go back to an unpublished graphic novel Boya wrote around 2015, is structured into three phases: *Walking Bread*, *Mill Singularity*, and *Breadverse*. *The Mill* is set in the fictional city of Chuldale Estate in the province of New Bread Republic. The gist of the story is that a corporation, confronted by food shortages and climate change (nothing at all like the real world!), creates synthetic bread. When eaten, though, the bread accidentally turns people into zombie-like creatures made of the same stuff. While the zombies are rather harmless, living people can't resist chewing on them, eventually turning themselves into zombies as well.

"It's an inverted zombie story where the living and zombie roles are flipped. It's kind of like a science fiction story," said Boya.

DOI: 10.1201/9781032683782-48

It's broadcast through a mosaic of animation bundles, which I call kinetic hieroglyphics, because it's not like, for example, YouTube, Instagram, or Netflix where you passively receive media. It's actually animation and other forms of storytelling that are appropriated by people to communicate in private or public conversations. So, it's like an inverted type of media where you're actively appropriating it as a user of these animations.

Confused? Well, let's start with Giphy. Giphy is the main organ of Boya's project. Everything begins there and then trickles down into other realms (NFTs, Tenor, Instagram, and eventually linear content for a series pitch).

Giphy appealed to Boya for a variety of reasons. "They are looping memes outside of linear storytelling and hence adequate for database storytelling," he said. "It's blockchain storytelling. It's decentralized and has its own autonomous production and marketing endeavors since it's strategically keyworded in the database and hyperlinked [url links to various storefronts] while also serving as a tool for communication and creative writing."

Boya met the Giphy folks back in 2014 when they were still a start-up company.

I used a lot of gifs on *Focus* [Boya's first film for the National Film Board of Canada] as a reference point. I realized that storytelling is migrating from the content realm to the database realm. So, this means less linear, more sculptural [viewed from different angles simultaneously outside of context].

In short, it's a modern variation of cubist painting.

Essentially then, *The Mill* channel is a non-linear pilot episode, a world-building project that can be seen from different angles simultaneously, almost like an interactive media place except that you're not a passive vessel in a contained space.

"The internet is the playground," he explained. "The way it's been seen, received, and socialized is effectively altering the material. People are investing energy in it. And then whenever it's seen, it's not being discovered, it's being recognized. That's the core of the operation."

Towards that end, some 50 plus artists (including the likes of Bill Plympton, Theodore Ushev, and the late Gary Leib) have been involved in contributing to *The Mill*. "Usually, I either invite an artist that I really love or sometimes people call me or text me about contributing," said Boya.

To get Plympton, Boya first showed him the channel. Different things happen on the channel, but it usually revolves around three characters: Bread Zombie, Aerodynamic Man (who has a turbine for a face like the character in Boya's short film, *Turbine*), and Fork Glasses. In the end, Plympton contributed a drawing of Bread Zombie and Aerodynamic Man.

"It's basically the cyber space version of street art, but more of an intervention and kind of like a popup that involves it," said Boya.

> It literally flattens the different distances between mediums and people's relationships to these mediums. It's really trying to break these hierarchies. It's kind of swimming against the current of what I would call industry tribalism, or even media tribalism, or just this idea that things are insulated. So specifically, it's different because these things are basically seen as sculptures. They're being seen from different angles.

In short, *The Mill* is not like a book or a film where you consume the story in a linear manner. Said Boya:

> It's basically intentional cultural appropriation on the part of the consumer of the content. I'm inviting them to appropriate it. So, it's inverting the idea that I have a story that is purely mine and that has to be unspoiled by appropriation.

Whatever Boya is doing, it certainly seems to have caught on. Aside from the 2.9 billion views on Giphy, *The Mill* has resonated with thousands of people. Just take a scroll along Boya's *Walking Bread* Facebook page and you'll see many posts featuring bread and turbine inspired images.

Boya believes the project has connected with people who

> belong to an ambiguous type of soft science fiction where interpretation and appropriation is embedded in their nature, like the xenomorph that adopts anatomy from the hosting animal. But really, all these people made this possible simply by caring about it.

Aside from just the creative reward, Boya is also making money. "There are multiple sources of income, but it's not for profit," he explained.

> It's cultural capital. I signed some forms that make it impossible to state publicly some of these sources, but essentially, consulting, production for UNESCO, and eventually several storefronts like NFTs from some gifs, physical artworks, etc. I'm also selling the actual creative process.

So, how does Boya envision *The Mill* unfolding?

> The first part is the ongoing Giphy channel. Secondly, there's the short film (*Bread Will Walk*) which will also serve as a pilot. *Bread Will Walk* will be a shorter version of the original graphic novel. Thirdly, a series, perhaps in the vein of *Love, Death, and Robots* on a platform like Crave or Netflix.

And what if the project doesn't evolve beyond the Giphy channel and short film?

"There will eventually be a brick-and-mortar museum around 2030, probably in Bulgaria," Boya predicts.

As for the world-building operation itself, I'm sort of doing a satire of what Disney is already doing very well. I want to make a *New Bread Republik* on a farm in Bulgaria with passports and sovereignty. Like *Burning Man*, but with farming and all sorts of strange rituals. Like the Hobbiton tourist site in New Zealand but more hardcore and dangerous.

Home Sick

The films of Michelle and Uri Kranot (2022)

49

"The ache for home lives in all of us, the safe place where we can go as we are and not be questioned," whispered a voice named Maya Angelou. Home is not some construction of bricks and glass; it's something deeper, something less visible than the material concepts of home that advertisers and assorted shills try to swindle us into believing. Home can't be bought and sold, but it sure as hell can be damaged. Home is a state of mind and being that is nurtured by love, companionship, connection, and safety. Unfortunately, there are those broken humans who lack those core traits and are dead set on destroying everyone else's sense of home.

The search for a home is central to Michelle and Uri Kranot's work. Throughout their impressive body of work, which addresses themes of injustice, war, corruption, racism, and exile, there is an overarching search for that safe place called home and a sense of community. Given that the Israeli-born, Denmark-based duo have first-hand experience of leaving their homeland to take roots elsewhere, it's not really a surprise.

In their earlier films, there's more of a focus on and concern with the destruction of home. The duo's first films (which you can see online), *God on Our Side* (2005) and *The Heart of Amos Klein* (2008), tackle the complex and senseless conflict between Israel and Palestine through, respectively, a pregnant woman whose unborn child is killed during a suicide bombing and a powerful Israeli army officer who reflects back on his life (and Israeli history) as he undergoes heart surgery. While *God on Our Side* uses cutout figures, *Klein* is the first of their films to start using mixed elements, notably drawings, paint, and live action.

   DOI: 10.1201/9781032683782-49

The Kranots then took a slightly new course with a fascinating trilogy (*White Tape, Black Tape, How Long Not Long*) that veers away from narrative and character-driven stories towards a more experimental, almost abstract exploration of concepts like boundaries, domination, and home. *Black Tape*, in particular, stands out for its clever and seductive use of tango to play off that old line: "It takes two to tango." It also takes two to occupy: the occupier and the occupied; the victim and the victimizer; the armed and the unarmed.

While these films focus primarily on the conflicts that cause one to lose their home, the more recent films have shifted, somewhat, from the visible conflict towards a search for a personal utopia and an acceptance that home, however imperfect, is where there is love and connection.

In *The Hollow Land* (2013), a couple struggles to adapt to their new home. In *Nothing Happens*, a crowd slowly gathers to watch an unseen event and becomes, perhaps, a community. Their more recent multi-disciplinary project, *The Hangman at Home* (2021), based on a poem by Carl Sandburg, continues that theme of community, disconnect, and watching, as we are allowed a glimpse into various moments of the inhabitants of an apartment building.

Visually, the Kranots, somewhat ironically, eschew the comforts of a familiar style and technique. They've dabbled with drawings, cutouts, puppets, paint, and live-action footage. They've made animated short films, but have also veered into VR and installations. Their narratives, rarely, if ever, linear, are fragmented, more like a fusion of poetry and fact, a swirling unpredictable loop of fact and fiction, past and present, political and personal. This uncertainty fuels the anxious fragility that seeps through each work and character as they strive forward in search of some sense of self and, with that, home.

F is for Flake
The (Not So) Great Animation Robbery? (2023)

50

Our little indie animation village is relatively small and, well, a bit boring. Most of the 'scandals' are limited to bitching about the Oscars, festival selections, and festival prizes. Occasionally, there is talk about inappropriate behaviour at festivals, but for the most part, it's a pretty calm and respectful landscape.

That all changed in late November 2022.

While attending the Animateka festival in Ljubljana, I got wind of a story spreading around. A film that had been accepted to several festivals was suddenly withdrawn. It was alleged that the film, *Away From Home*, directed by Brunella De Cola, was a copy of Natalia Chernysheva's 2012 short, *The Snowflake* (which we screened at the Ottawa International Animation Festival in 2013). I didn't pay much attention to the story because I was in the haze of festival mode and suffering from symptoms of what would turn out to be my second brief non-love affair with COVID.

Back home, though, in the midst of COVID restlessness, I started reading a bit more about the story and quickly became mystified by it. Maybe it was the result of spending a part of my childhood with a stepfather who was a detective, but anyway, I suddenly felt quite fascinated with this story and determined to find some semblance of truth. A scandal of this magnitude – hell, of any magnitude – is pretty much alien to our little village of indie animation shorts. In my 30 years, I have not heard of such a thing allegedly (you'll hear that word a lot) happening.

I contacted Anna Gaschutz at the Dresden Film Festival. They were the festival that first raised a red flag.

DOI: 10.1201/9781032683782-50

I first saw only a glimpse of the film [*Away from Home*] when my colleague was watching it and I mentioned *Snowflake* to her. My colleague said it's not [*Snowflake*], so I first thought that the director had made a new film in a similar style. However, then our kid's-programme manager watched the film in the submissions and wrote to the team that it is the same film as *Snowflake*... So, I watched it and checked out *Snowflake* again, and indeed, it was the same film.

Gaschutz eventually wrote to the short's distribution company, Zen Movie. "They were super shocked and didn't know about it, and they immediately spoke to the producer and took all the legal steps they needed to," adds Gaschautz. "I am also quite surprised someone would do this."

While Zen Movie and A Little Confidence (the film's producers) were reluctant to comment on the situation given that De Cola is adamant that she did not steal the film and is pursuing legal avenues, it's clear that they are quite floored by the whole situation. They took De Cola at her word when she presented the final film to them.

On December 5, the two companies issued a statement:

> *This joint statement is signed by Zen Movie and A Little Confidence, respectively as Distributor and 'Producer'/Agent of the animated short film* Away from Home. *Zen Movie and A Little Confidence first and foremost express their absolute extraneousness and profound surprise about what they have acknowledged on November 28th, 2022 regarding the dispute over the right's ownership of the short film, raised by a third party.*
>
> *On April 19th, 2022, Ms. Brunella De Cola provided the Agent with the short film which was already complete, fully realized in all of its parts, giving full guarantees that she was its producer, author and director, while only later did the Agent propose to Zen Movie to take care of the festival career of the short film; Zen Movie, after watching the short film, accepted such assignment and located the work in its catalog called 'Tiny Distribution.'*
>
> *In specifying that Ms. Brunella De Cola is still affirming herself as the owner of the rights of the film, the undersigned, given the adverse revindications, have decided to immediately stop the distribution of the short film and to withdraw all the submissions already made to festivals. The undersigned, insofar as it is within their respective competencies, will adopt, in every area of their activity, the most appropriate solutions in order to shed light on the effective chain of rights of the short film and, if necessary, will take any further action aimed at protecting their interests and professional reputation.*

Chernysheva first learned of the new film while at work at Folimage animation studio:

"Folimage is the distributor of my film in France" They told me that someone in the committee of Clermont Ferrand Film Festival recognized the problem. *Snowflake* is well known in France and in fact it was selected for the competition program in the very same festival 10 years ago. At first I thought it was a joke. I don't know Brunella De Cola. We have never met.

Now, initially, I had not seen the *Away From Home* version, so I was trying to keep a somewhat open mind. One story that passed by my ears was that De Cola was claiming that 10 years ago or so she'd participated in a free course or workshop at the French school, ESMA. De Cola is allegedly claiming that the original material was first created during this course/workshop, and that Natalia Chernysheva was also part of this workshop group and used the material for her film, *The Snowflake* without the permission of other students.

If that's true, that there was such an event, why did it take 10 years for this issue to arise? Was De Cola perhaps not even aware that *The Snowflake* existed?

In an email from January 10, 2023, a representative from ESMA told me, "After consulting our old student lists, we could not find any name corresponding or close to Brunella de Cola."

Chernysheva, meanwhile, is adamant that she has never met De Cola nor has she ever stepped foot inside any ESMA campus (she was a student at La Poudrière in France).

Eventually, I managed to see a copy of *Away from Home*. It was clear that except for the title and end credits, this was all footage that was used in *The Snowflake*. It has the same soundtrack and virtually the same running time. So, the notion that De Cola was not aware (if this story about a workshop is true) of the existence of *The Snowflake* is certainly suspect at this point. Also, in the credits, the music was credited to Lorenzo Petruzziello even though this version of *Away from Home* has the same soundtrack as *The Snowflake*.

The mystery deepens.

After doing some intensive amateur investigating with the help of some colleagues, a public Facebook post (that has since been removed) by Petruzziello was sent to me. In the post, he talks about making music for the project:

> I'm really happy about the success Brunella De Cola's animated short for my track 'Away From Home' is getting. They played with me the masters Lucio D'Amato on piano and Marco de Tilla on double bass, expertly recorded and missed by the great Marco Ruggiero.

What caught my eye was the mention of a piano being used as an instrument. There is no piano in either the *Away from Home* or *The Snowflake* versions I saw.

Then, someone sent me a YouTube link (that, you guessed it, has since been removed) where Petruzziello posted a version of *Away from Home* with his score. Aside from his soundtrack (which jives with what he wrote in his Facebook post), it was the same 'Away from Home' that I saw, containing what seems to be the same footage as *The Snowflake.*

As a result, we now have two versions of *Away from Home.* How? Why?

Meanwhile, in the December 2020 issue of the Italian magazine *Scenografia&Costume*, De Cola is interviewed about her new short animation film, *Away from Home* (pg. 57, *Scenografia&Costume*, n. 18 - Dicembre 2020). *When asked about the origins of her project, she says:*

> *Lorenzo Petruzziello, my drum teacher, sent me a piece of his called* Away from Home, *asking me to make a video for this jazz composition he had recorded. During the period we were all forced to stay at home, I wondered what could be a way to take a trip, to visit places far away from us. So I thought of an African child who, unlike us, does not really have the means to move around the world; he does not have the possibility, for example, of seeing a snowy valley or a big city.*

This certainly differs from the story that all this material was created in a workshop 10 years earlier.

If *Away from Home* is a plagiarized version of *The Snowflake*, one wonders why anyone would do this. Some anti-Russian business? (Given that De Cola was interviewed about the film in December 2020, that theory doesn't quite make sense since the invasion of Ukraine happened in early 2022). Did someone make up the name or use De Cola's name without her knowledge? (Again, that's unlikely given that De Cola travelled with the film to the POFF festival in Estonia this year and even did a video interview – since removed – about the film). Was it a way to get funding? Mental health issues? What could the endgame possibly be?

De Cola has not helped her cause within the animation community. She's not known in the world of animation festivals or the indie animation community. Her credits are more connected with television and feature films. That's certainly not evidence of any wrongdoing, but rather than simply issuing a statement that openly addresses the controversy, she chose to write a Facebook post (since removed) claiming she'd been slandered and that she had hired a lawyer to sort the matter out (and, in fact, ASIFA-International recently received a letter from said lawyer warning them not to denounce De Cola until all that facts have been unveiled).

And, that's fair. Innocent until proven otherwise.

Also, Chernysheva is a known and respected artist in the animation community who has made a handful of films since *The Snowflake* and has a fairly recognizable style and voice. She has been quite open and public about the issue.

I want to stop the distribution of this forgery at festivals and online. I have ample proof at my disposal. First, it was my graduation project. It was produced one year after university by studio Pchela in Moscow in 2012. Secondly, my teachers, friends and collaborators can all bear witness to the fact that I was the creator and director of *Snowflake*.

With both parties adamant that they are in the right, it seems that it will be left to legal avenues to sort this bizarre situation out. Whatever unfolds, this controversy will surely serve as a wake-up call to the animation community.

Neither Brunella de Cola nor Lorenzo Petruzziello responded when asked to comment on the situation.

"The truth," my granny once told me after she saw me take Christmas cookies from her jar and I denied it, "is rarely pure and never simple."

Georges Schwizgebel

51

Galloping Towards the Abyss (2018)

Bursting with inviting colours, sounds, and imagery, Georges Schwizgebel is the consummate animator. Each frame is a work of art, intricately timed, painted, edited and scored. There is simply no one in animation like Schwizgebel. He is an artist who consistently creates unique and groundbreaking techniques, whose innovation soars beyond the radar of the best dreams of the finest animators.

There's a romantic, nostalgic, almost classical vibe to the Swiss animator's work. Placed from a distant, fleeting viewpoint, almost like birds flying by a neighbourhood, we watch his characters roam through real and imagined mental and physical landscapes, remembering, desiring, fleeing and pursuing. There is music, dancing, loving, tasting, and playing as the characters breathlessly breathe while galloping alongside the brevity of being, absorbing mementoes of experiences and sensations along the way.

Yet, seeping beneath the surface of these warm and lush palettes and sounds, and the many pastoral scenarios, is a constant sense of melancholy that borders on dread. Throughout Schwizgebel's work (e.g., *La Course a l' Abîme*, *L' Année Du Daim*, *L' Homme Sans Ombre*, *Erlkönig*), there are constant reminders of the abyss, the exit that awaits us all.

But rather than embracing that darkness, Schwizgebel encourages us to savour as much as we can. He encourages us to accept and appreciate the fragility of this whole thing and to dive in and devour every good, bad and shitty slice of life that comes our way before the colours fade and the music stops.

Crossing the Rubicon

52

Remembering Gil Alkabetz (2023)

> *What are these dark days I see? / In this world so*
> *badly bent / I cannot redeem the time*
> *The time so idly spent / How much longer can it*
> *last? / How long can it go on? /*
> *I embrace my love, put down my hair / And I*
> *crossed the Rubicon*
> Bob Dylan – *Crossing the Rubicon*

To say it was a shock would be a gross understatement. When word spread in September 2022 that the gentle, Israeli-born, German-based animator Gil Alkabetz had taken his life, few could reconcile the news. Unknown to many of his colleagues in the animation circuit, Alkabetz had battled depression for much of his life. Clearly, it reached a point where he felt there was no better way to silence the black dog than to end his life, and with it, what must have been constant dark noise.

Is it too much that I'm writing this with bluntness? There was a time when suicide was hushed, limited to discreet whispers. As if it were some kind of sin, some kind of weakness. Such nonsense, frankly. A decade ago, a childhood friend of mine took her own life. During the funeral, there was awkwardness. Everyone knew, but no one wanted to say it.

But we need to talk about it. We need to almost normalize it so that we can get away from stigmatizing mental illness. That doesn't mean Gil could have been saved. I have no idea what was going through his mind. No one really

DOI: 10.1201/9781032683782-52

does, but perhaps if he were able to be more open about these inner demons, maybe, just maybe, he'd still be here firing off his brilliant Instagram cartoons while gifting us with more of his unique animation films.

Once upon a time, I had intended to write about Alkabetz's work. For whatever reason, that didn't happen. I did, however, find a file that contained the beginnings of an interview I was doing with Alkabetz. It's undated, but likely from around 2011. I've incorporated his thoughtful and enlightening responses into the brief overview of his work below.

Gil Alkabetz was one of the masters in the animation community. He made films that rarely looked the same, yet there was never any doubt about who made them. Whether he was making kids' films (*Trim Time, A Sunny Day*), commissioned pieces (the opening credits for the feature, *Run Lola Run),* or more experimental exercises (*Da Vinci Time Code*), Alkabetz's voice was always recognizable.

Animation fascinated Alkabetz from the moment memory kicked in:

In my childhood in Israel, watching animation was quite a rare experience: TV started only when I was 10 years old, and I used to watch cartoons on my neighbour's 8-mm projector. There was a magical sensation about it, and ever since then, animation has been connected, for me, with magic. Even today, the very fact that drawn figures could walk still fascinates me. I believe that every animator would admit to being constantly surprised by the mysterious emerging of movement out of a series of static images.

Alkabetz's work frequently played with narrative, often eschewing linear narrative in favour of a playful approach that sometimes unfolds like a cross between a non-linear experimental work and a thriller (i.e., *Yankale, Morir de Amor, 1+1*). "Narrative has always been the most difficult part for me in making a film," Alkabetz wrote to me.

In short films in general and in animation in particular, there must always be something extraordinary. Since I am usually keeping my design simple, it has to be something in the story or in the concept. Finding a concept is extremely difficult for me. In a way, it is like inventing the wheel every time again.

In terms of influences, Paul Driessen – who also playfully tinkered with narrative and space – was a major influence on Alkabetz – seems to have been an influence on your work (humour, themes, playing with space, and narrative). "Driessen, together with Caroline Leaf, were my first exposure to a non-Disney-like animation," said Alkabetz.

Driessen's film *Cat's Cradle* made a huge impression on me back then. I guess one can see the influence of this film, as well as Caroline Leaf's films, on my first film, *Bitzbutz* (1985). I admire Driessen's ability to blend logic with fantasy: it reminds me of one of my favourite authors, Lewis Carroll. I, personally, often feel I am too tied to logic, and I envy animators who can free themselves from it (like the Estonian filmmakers, for example). Still, I need to have a logical basis for my films, and this is what I have always admired in Paul Driessen's fantastic creation.

Since his debut in 1984 (with the student film, *Bitz Butz*), his best films – tinged with dry humour – frequently manipulate space and explore the boundaries of narrative as they ponder identity, war, and human nature.

Swamp (1991) is a satire on the idiocy of war, featuring two opposing armies. Each mounted soldier is armed with giant scissors and kept from tumbling into the nothingness of an unseen swamp by a large balloon. The inevitable ending bursts the notion that war can ever really have winners and heroes.

In the minimalist mystery, *Yankale* (1995), Alkabetz cleverly manipulates space and framing while constructing a non-linear tale of a Kafkaesque-type character who decides to temporarily flee an overbearing mother and the tedious routine of his life.

After *Morir de Amor* (2005) (a hilarious work about two parrots singing about their troubled past), *Rubicon* (1997) is probably Alkabetz's most popular film. It's an easy one to like. Here, the animator promises to solve an old riddle that, paradoxically, he has no intention of solving. Instead, the riddle offers Alkabetz an excuse to play around with space while cheekily exploring the problematic and often impossible relationship between the theoretical and the actual. Oh, and it's also very funny.

1+1 (2015) remains one of my favourites by Alkabetz. Divided into seven parts, this existential thriller, with echoes of Paul Auster, uses only seven different images. Stylistically, it harkens back to *Yankele* (the central character even shares the same cross-shaped traits). With its minimal imagery and limited movement, *1+1* unfurls a respectful but teasing middle finger to animations that drown in a flood of drawings, design, and movement.

So here we are. Shall I end with the usual attempt at positivity, some cliche about how we might have lost the man but we still hear him through his art? Somehow, that's not enough.

Sigh Soothing
The films of Xi Chen and Xu An (2023)

53

Combining a love of silent films, Chinese art, theatre, and stop motion with a hint of animator Igor Kovalyov's design and unique pacing (think Robert Bresson if you know that name better), Xi Chen's poetic and personal films (frequently made in collaboration with the late Xu An) explore individual stories of love, loss, and lust, while offering insights into historical and contemporary Chinese society.

Chen's introduction to animation came via, of all things, *The Smurfs*. "I was very young, maybe seven years old. After I saw that on TV, I hoped to one day be a person who can also make animation like that."

After majoring in Administrative Management at university, Chen began tinkering with flash software and making his own animation works. Eventually, he enrolled in the Beijing Film Academy to get a master's degree in animation.

A turning point in Chen's creative direction happened in 2005 at the Ottawa International Animation Festival.

> I watched Igor Kovalyov's *Milch* at the festival. I think this is the animated short film that has the most important influence on me. This work inspired me, for example, in terms of narrative, film language. In terms of aesthetics, as well as the aesthetics of using animation to express a certain neurotic person, I gradually discovered that I have a lot of things I want to express in these aspects. Before that, I didn't know that these things could be expressed and were worth expressing.

DOI: 10.1201/9781032683782-53

During that time, Chen met his creative partner, Xu An. They met while working for an animation studio that was churning out TV animation. From the start, the two have similar interests and quickly became friends. Soon, they started to collaborate on their own films. "We both felt at the time that this collaboration would result in higher quality work," says Chen. "We have been making animated short films together since 2008, but unfortunately, he was diagnosed with cancer in 2014, and he passed away in 2017. After that, I worked on the rest of our projects."

The films often find their genesis in ancient paintings or photos.

> I will imagine the living conditions and interpersonal relationships of the people in them. This kind of imagination gives me great inspiration and passion. The temperament of the people in older times is very different from the people in today's life. This difference really interests me. Our animation short film is to realize these stories, which is extremely exciting for us and actually soothes and heals our hearts.

A key ingredient that links all of the films is the Chinese lunar calendar. "At the beginning of this series, I felt that the fate of people and the changes of solar terms were secretly connected," says Chen. "There are 24 solar terms every year. The Chinese name of each film is the name of a solar term."

Early films like *The Winter Solstice* (2008), *A Clockwork Cock* (2009) and *The Grain Coupon* (2011), armed with that strange 'Kovalyovian' pacing, all show an interest in narrative exploration and experimentation. In *Winter Solstice*, a man is shot. As he dies, he revisits an old lover. In *Clockwork Cock*, a schoolboy is punished by his teacher. *Grain Coupon* is the most ambitious story, following the conflicts between an older couple and a menacing soldier.

Despite the historical setting (1920s China), *The Winter Solstice* is entirely fictional. "At that time," says Chen, "I was more interested in people's near-death experience, and sex and death were difficult to separate."

The elliptical narrative is presented almost as a series of silent tableaus offering the viewers only vague hints about what might be unfolding before them. It's left to us to fill in any gaps. Visually, the distinct graphic design is enhanced by shaky, unstable camera work, aptly mirrors the dying man's fading memories.

A Clockwork Cock follows a similar path. While the setting is a teacher's office and a schoolyard, the relationship between the student and teacher can also be read as that of individual versus state. The boy is curious, fascinated by insects, by the wonders and freedom of nature. The teacher is more rigid. She follows the rules and has portraits of Stalin and Mao on the wall. It's also a jab at the school system which often destroys curiosity and individuality as it slowly imposes societal rules and expectations. The boy, like so many, will be swallowed up by the prevailing social system; a tendency not unique to China.

The Grain Coupon is rooted in the Chinese Cultural Revolution (1966–1976). A grain rationing system was imposed by the government in the 1950s to control food production and boost industry. People were given coupons to buy a set amount (which varied depending on age, profession and location) of grain at a low price. Naturally, restrictions are exploited, manipulated and mis-used. Fusing history, melodrama and comedy, a debilitated old man (who lives with his seamstress wife) offers his snuff bottle to a soldier in exchange for a grain coupon. The soldier refuses, instead asking the man to forge a precious stamp. It does not go well! The old man's sigh that ends the film is a perfect summation of the absurdity of his time and existence.

Grain Coupon is the duo's most ambitious work to date. What's particularly striking is how they limit the almost 20-minute film to a single setting. In earlier and later films, the films are often limited to a single space (e.g., *The Swallow*, *A Fly in the Restaurant*) or minimal spaces. "With *Grain Coupon*, says Chen,

> we wanted to try a single-scene animation, and at that time we were very interested in the history of the Chinese Cultural Revolution, and felt that it was so absurd and magical. This story is also purely fictional, and it also comes from our understanding of the experience of reading historical docu-ments of this period.

Chen's films are graphically diverse, often the result of experimentation. "These graphic styles were generally the ones I was most interested in at the time. I wanted to try out the effects in animation, and I gradually explored one after another." Flash software also often dictated the graphic direction. "The software is very suitable for making cutout animations, and it is a flat space, which is also very close to the traditional oriental art style," adds Chen. "For a period of time, An Xu and I tried to avoid zooming in and zooming out, as well as film photography languages like montage, and always wanted to use methods that looked like paintings."

Beginning with *Grain Coupon* and especially their next film, *Mahjong*, there's a notable shift award from narrative towards an interest in experiment-ing with space and time. In a Chinese-style garret (i.e., a small and not very comfortable room), four men play mahjong. They play and drink as a woman stands nearby in silence, holding a bottle of liquor. As the game unfolds (and the alcohol consumed) the suppressed cravings of each character begin to sur-face. Things then get a bit nuts. "At that time," adds Chen, "we were very dis-appointed with the situation in China and felt that we were living in an animal world."

The design has a more faint, fragile look than early films. Each player is almost transparent, as if between life and death (or in this case, animal and human). The story – which came from a Chinese folk woodblock print that showed three monkeys playing mahjong against a pig – is framed and presented like live theatre. Space and time overlap. We're never entirely sure where or when we are. "We borrowed from the art style of Chinese shadow puppetry," says Chen. "We also wanted to explore some animation film languages, such as using translucency, light, and stillness to highlight a character. Grab the viewer's attention for a split second instead of using montage."

The Swallow (2014) is a beautiful and modest old-school portrait of three generations of Chinese women. The film is set in what might be a room of a larger house or just a small domestic space that the three women share. Without words – and apparently from the perspective of a passing swallow just outside the window – Chen nimbly captures the distances between the generations: the traditional grandmother versus the modern mother versus the abandoned granddaughter.

At times, the combination of black and white, old music, theatre and a jittery image convince you that you're watching a film made in the 1930s. The unstable, wavy image makes it feel as though you're watching the film in an impromptu ballroom theatre of a ship.

With no words, minimal mise-en-scène (the film never moves from the centre of the main room, even when there is a point where the characters all leave 'us' alone in the room; it's a wonderful moment in the film that creates suspense and bemusement), instead relying entirely on simple character gestures, Chen tells a tale of a troubled family and with it, shifting attitudes in contemporary China.

The Poem (2015) is a moving fresco that follows travellers in search of a plum blossom during a harsh winter storm. The plum blossom is often a symbol of hope following a long winter. In this context, it feels more like a symbol for rebirth, perhaps a metaphor for existence or a specific period in Chinese history. Hope for change or growth, a search for some semblance of paradise after scouring the daily storms of existence.

A Fly in the Restaurant (2018) is a mesmerizing cutout film set in a local restaurant. Told from what seems to be the perspective of a rotating ceiling fan, the film follows the interior and exterior action as a cook chases a fly, and a variety of patrons (soldiers, hunters, artists, men, women) mingle, sleep, eat, and come and go. Along the wall of the restaurant is a slogan that translates as "Revolution Is not a Dinner Party."

Mixing shades of red for the exteriors with dirtier, greyer interior colours (depicting a dreary daily existence), *A Fly in the Restaurant* is a not-so-subtle critique of a complacent populace ensconced in a Chinese landscape in constant political and social flux.

Ironically, the only character with any life and purpose seems to be the fly – and everyone wants to kill it.

The Six (2019) veers even deeper into non-linear narrative and spatial and temporal exploration, creating a mesmerizing piece of animated poetry. This one involves a sort of dance between a man, woman, and crane that is repeated six times.

Chen's most recent film, *The Loach* (2021) is a haunting silent film that combines eye-popping cutout designs with a mysterious, elliptical narrative to create a ghostly mini-melodrama nightmare that touches upon themes of gender, class, materialism and child-rearing in contemporary Chinese society.

Independently-orientated animation has been on the rise in China over the last decade or so. Far removed from the family features or tepid TV shows, there has been a consistently impressive body of work that shows a willingness to experiment. For Chen, making independent art is not difficult in China if you keep your budget low and time short. Even then, getting the film distributed and shown remains a challenge (as it is for indie animators worldwide). The bigger obstacle facing Chinese animators – to no one's surprise – censorship. "Censorship remains a major problem including self-censorship and official censorship," says Chen. "Gradually this will limit thinking, and worse, you will get unconsciously used to it."

Chen's work, in some ways, reminds me of the way Estonian artists worked in the Soviet Union days. The so-called absurdist nature of Estonian animators was arguably developed during the Soviet days as a way to sneak their messages and criticisms into a story. Chen's films are by no means absurdist (though they have their moments), but the uniqueness and power of the work stems from its multi-layered meanings. By focusing on domestic settings and individual stories, the personal and social merge. The reality and chaos of individual lives cannot possibly hide surrounding social and political realities. They will always seep into the picture. The emphasis on individuals along with recognizable genres and art forms (e.g., melodrama, theatre) also extends the themes and stories beyond the walls of China. You don't need a Chinese passport to understand the desires, cravings, fears, and missteps of the characters. We've all been there, all had a moment where in the face of utter calamity, all we can do is sit back and take a big, long and deeply exasperated – yet strangely calming – sigh.

A Change Comin' On

54

Exploring the Mindscapes of Masaaki Yuasa

> *Gonna change my way of thinking/Make myself a*
> *different set of rules*
> *Going to put my good foot forward/Stop being*
> *influenced by fools*
> – Bob Dylan

"Who am I?I?I?" roared (allegedly) the great Eastern metaphysicist, Jackie Chan, atop a hill not far from Kyoto, not long after binge-watching the animation works of the Japanese mindsculptor, Masaaki Yuasa.

I get it. Whether it's feature films (*Mind Game, The Night Is Short, Walk on Girl, Inu-Oh*), short films (*Kick-Heart*), series (*Ping Pong, Tatami Galaxy, Devilman Crybaby*), or one-off television episodes (*Adventure Time, Space Dandy*), Yuasa's unhinged, gonzo-tinged brainscapes dazzle and dizzy you into questioning who, what, and where you really are. A collision between coming-of-age stories, Looney Tunes, philosophy, and surrealism, Yuasa's kaleidoscopic dances burst with visual madness, rapid-fire colour patterns, sudden shifts in character design, and elastic character movements. Imaginative, magical, and original.

"I love both Tex Avery and Dali," admits Yuasa.

DOI: 10.1201/9781032683782-54

I've been influenced by a lot of artists, and I get inspired by a lot of things I see, hear, smell, and touch in everyday life. I believe anything that inspires me could be turned into anime. Actually, the structure of tunes can be a model for storyboards when working on them. I often derive inspiration even from really modest visuals: a commercial, a cut from a movie, a movement from an anime, as well as nameless flowers and grasses blooming on the road, clouds, stars, and moons in the sky. I'm also inspired by what I'm currently interested in and feeling. My humble wish for creating anime is to have common images, conversations, and scenes sublimed into artworks.

Impossible is possible in Yuasa's world. There are no laws of physics. Yuasa births worlds and people that are stylized, exaggerated, distorted, and impossibly possible. Along the way, his works explore truths about individuals, relationships and society. Unlike some artists, Yuasa doesn't beat us over the head with messages and weighty themes. He lets the audience breathe. There are mysteries unexplained, left for us to ponder, make sense of, or walk away from. Every episode, say, of the extraordinary series *Tatami Galaxy* (2010) is a standalone work of art that rivals any indie animation short. In it, he takes a fairly common theme of feckless post-secondary students on campus and turns it into an utterly surreal, time-shifting portrait of students, identity, fate, community, and society.

Throughout all of Yuasa's work (whether it's the bizarre Romeo and Juliet meets flesh-eating monsters series, *Kemonozume* or the high school table tennis melodrama, *Ping Pong*), we encounter anxious young people sifting through life in search of a worthy purpose or at the very least a meaningful connection. It wouldn't be stretching it to say that the many characters who populate Yuasa's universe wouldn't be out of place in the philosophical books of Kierkegaard, who, in a different medium and manner, wrote in shifting tones, voices, names, and styles (much like Yuasa's work makes frequent shifts in time, space, design, and style) as he attempted to sort out the question of how one lives.

In Yuasa's widely beloved *Mind Game* (2004), Nishi is an aspiring artist who ends up getting his ass shot all the way to limbo, where he manages to get a second chance at life and correct his fatal mistake and thus his cowardly demeanour. In the end, Nishi's fate is open-ended. He's certainly acted with more compassion for others, but is the end result going to be any different?

Tatami Galaxy (2010), a brilliant unofficial precursor to *The Night is Short, Walk on Girl* (2017), follows a senior at Kyoto University who travels through parallel universes so he can see how his life might have changed if he'd joined a particular student club. Much like Nishi's fate in *Mind Game*, the unnamed student soon realizes that there is no right choice and no perfect life.

In the short film *Kick-Heart* (2013), a seemingly irreconcilable duality exists when a wrestler finds himself torn between loving a rival wrestler, Lady S, and a nun. He soon learns that these two worlds are not so different after all.

Although widely different in terms of tone, style, and intended audience, the features *Lu Over the Wall* (2017) and *Night is Short* are ultimately about love, kindness, and acceptance—themes that we all need to be reminded of in this somewhat erratic time of intolerance.

"*Lu Over the Wall* is a story about a mermaid who just wishes to make good friends with human beings," says Yuasa.

> It's about overcoming an irrational sense of discrimination and prejudice, about understanding and accepting alien creatures. Similarly, *Night is Short* is a fable about how you'll only be happy when you wish for someone's happiness and you'll be unhappy when you just wish for your own happiness. Both movies depict how coming out of your shell could make things better. I love stories about opening up your heart.

In the masterful series *Devilman Crybaby* (2018), based on Go Nagai's 1972 manga series *Devilman*, a race of ancient demons wants to eradicate humanity. A rich and odd young man named Ryo convinces his friend Akira to unite with a demon so that he can become a Devilman and gain the powers of a demon while retaining his human sense of compassion and love. Beyond all the gore and explicit sex is a smart, striking, and multi-layered story that fuses coming-of-age themes and social issues (racism, sexism, urban violence) with generally despicable human behaviours. *Devilman Crybaby* asks difficult questions about good and bad. It's a story about us and our insatiable greed, desire, and nastiness.

In Yuasa's world, nothing is black and white. There are no outright good or bad people. There are just people who make good and bad decisions. Then again, how do we know if a decision is good or bad until we've made it? "It seems easy to be a good person or a bad person, but it is difficult to remain a good person," says Yuasa.

> I would like to show that change is very easy for each and every one of us, and I think it is interesting that it is not possible. In fact, it is difficult to change the world, but it is easy to change one's own worldview by changing oneself.

Space and time are frequently manipulated and warped in Yuasa's works, perhaps mirroring the discombobulated states of the characters. In a 2017 interview with the Fantasia International Film Festival, Yuasa said:

> I try to show the landscape that the characters see subjectively, not objectively. For example, if they see something that does not exist, I will make it

appear, or if something vanishes in the environment or in space, I erase it.
So, I think if things become less rigid and lighter, I will see space like that.
It's intimately linked to emotions.

In a sense, it's a breakdown between the conscious and subconscious, as though we're witnessing both the external and internal states of the character.

In the ingenious short, *Happy Machine* (part of the 2007 anthology feature *Genius Party*), this Dalí-inspired piece is a haunting, moving, and trippy take on coming of age, seen through the eyes of a baby. Through the baby's unformed eyes and mind, we encounter a bizarre, Dalíesque landscape where everyday objects take on dangerous and otherworldly appearances. It's like Yuasa interpreted Jacques Lacan's mirror stage theory (the idea that babies initially see themselves as one with the world until the moment they see themselves in the mirror). For Lacan, this is when subjectivity and desire begin. He argued that we spend the rest of our lives trying to get back to that pre-mirror state. *Happy Machine* is a perfect example of the way Yuasa creates subjective spaces that mirror the character's state of being.

A distorted sense of time also runs rampant through all of Yuasa's films. It can be both unnerving and liberating for the characters. In *Mind Game*, *Tanami Galaxy*, and *Night is Short*, there is a sense of neverending time, yet the characters quickly discover that it does not necessarily provide any more clarity. At times, it's like there is a race with and against time. That we must make use of every second, minute, and hour. The protagonist in *Tanami Galaxy* feels he's wasted two years and thinks that different choices would have led to a "rose-coloured campus life." He doesn't realize that it doesn't work that way, that he was not wasting his time, and that every experience and choice, no matter how seemingly trivial, has value if you're paying attention. A similar theme runs through *Night is Short*. If you're open to it, there are always new experiences waiting for you. In all three works, finding a semblance of identity and inner stability involves being present, compassionate, and selfless.

Music has always been an important part of Yuasa's work. In *Lu over the Wall*, music is what bridges not just the island community but also the world between the merfolk and humans. It's the music that brings out the dancing feet in everyone, including Lu. Here, Yuasa shows us the power that music can have in breaking down borders and uniting.

Yuasa's most recent feature, *Inu-Oh* (2022), also brings music to the forefront of what must be his most unconventional film. Part history of a forgotten Noh performer (the mysterious Inu-Oh), part *Hedwig and the Angry Inch*, *Inu-Oh* is a riveting and unique experience (especially when audiences are energetically involved, dancing and stomping while waving their glowsticks to the rhythm of each song, as they did during a screening at the 2022 Hiroshima Animation Festival).

Along the way, Yuasa explores familiar themes (youth, friendship, identity) while mashing up timelines. When the deformed Inu-Oh hooks up with the blind biwa player, Tomona, the two form an alliance that propels them to rock superstardom in 14th-century Japan. The result is a weird and wild blend of modern-day rock, ancient instruments, and Noh dance that touches upon themes of tolerance and notions of history.

Yuasa's ambitions seem multifold; he is not only celebrating ancient art forms in Japan, but also challenging our notions of history. Aside from the heavy metal/glam look of the various bands, there's even a scene where Tomona plays his biwa behind the back of his head, à la Jimi Hendrix. "In modern times, we think of dances and music as things we created, but they could have appeared in the past too. Maybe there was someone playing a biwa thousands of years ago like Jimi Hendrix."

Maybe music is the key to the soul, to love, truth, and all that good stuff. "It is a pleasure that has been around since ancient times and has no negative effects on people," says Yuasa.

> I think people from all walks of life can enjoy it together because the differences in the languages each person can use don't seem to matter for the sake of enjoyment. If we can find a way to enjoy any kind of music, I think the world will expand and become more enjoyable.

So, dear Jackie Chan, next time you're struggling through your dour days, shouting on a hilltop, remember: music, love, and time-wasting are all you really need for a decent life.

Index

Printed in the United States
by Baker & Taylor Publisher Services